A QUALITY SYSTEM
FOR EDUCATION

Also available from Quality Press

TQM: A Step-by-Step Guide to Implementation
Charles N. Weaver, PhD

The Quality Promise
Lester Jay Wollschlaeger

An Approach to Quality Improvement That Works, Second Edition
A. Donald Stratton

Management Excellence Through Quality
Thomas J. Barry

The Quest for Quality in Services
A. C. Rosander

Baldrige Award Winning Quality
Mark Graham Brown

Leadership, Perspective, and Restructuring for Total Quality
Richard J. Pierce, editor

Quality: The Myth and the Magic
Cynthia Lane Westland

The Quality Master Plan
J. P. Russell

A Leader's Journey to Quality
Dana Cound

To request a complimentary catalog of publications,
call 800-248-1946.

A QUALITY SYSTEM FOR EDUCATION

Using Quality and Productivity Techniques
to Save Our Schools

Stanley J. Spanbauer

With the assistance of Jo Hillman
In cooperation with the faculty and staff
of the Fox Valley Technical College

ASQC Quality Press
Milwaukee, Wisconsin

A QUALITY SYSTEM FOR EDUCATION

Stanley J. Spanbauer

Library of Congress Cataloging-in-Publication Data

Spanbauer, Stanley J.
    A quality system for education: using quality and productivity
techniques to save our schools/Stanley J. Spanbauer; with the
assistance of Jo Hillman; in cooperation with the faculty and
staff of the Fox Valley Technical College.
      p. cm.
    Includes bibliographical references (p.) and index.
    ISBN 0-87389-156-2
    1. Education, Higher—United States. 2. Quality Control—United
      States.   I. Hillman, Jo Ann.   II. Title.
LA227.4.S63   1992
378.73—dc20   91-44489
                                              CIP

1098765432

ISBN 0-87389-156-2

Acquisitions Editor: Jeanine L. Lau
Production Editor: Mary Beth Nilles
Marketing Administrator: Susan Westergard
Set in 10-point Palatino by Patricia L. Coogan.
Cover design by Wayne Dober.
Printed and bound by BookCrafters.

For a free copy of the ASQC Quality Press Publications
Catalog, including ASQC membership information, call
800-248-1946.

Printed in the United States of America

 Printed on Acid-Free Recycled Paper

 ASQC
Quality Press
611 East Wisconsin Avenue
Milwaukee, Wisconsin 53202

To the faculty, staff, and students of Fox Valley Technical College. Their enthusiasm for and commitment to excellence is the impetus for innovation which has distinguished the college.

And to the Fox Valley Technical College District Board of Education. Their dedication, support, and willingness to take risks has created an environment that fosters continual growth.

CONTENTS

ILLUSTRATIONS

PREFACE

When we first initiated quality processes at Fox Valley Technical College (FVTC) six years ago, there were skeptics who wondered whether incorporating the techniques and methods of quality and productivity, and using industrial models in the design of curriculum and scheduling and delivery of instruction, would work in the complex environment of schools.

I must admit that I was apprehensive myself. I knew that it would be relatively easy to use these techniques with service department employees, such as bookstore workers, secretaries, custodians, maintenance staff, and all those who perform functions similar to those found in the private sector.

But I wasn't quite sure if these concepts would be accepted by teachers—the heart and soul of the educational process. While we have had general success fostering change at FVTC, there has always been some resistance to change, at least from a vocal minority. I've learned, over the years, that this limited opposition to quick change has been good for the organization. Teachers can't be blamed for being wary of new projects and innovations that are regularly foisted on them. Typically, new initiatives have come and gone, usually replaced by a new idea, hailed as the panacea to cure the ills of education.

For some reason, the quality/productivity movement at FVTC has been different. While there are still critics, general acceptance is exceptional! Throughout the college, discussions about quality echo loudly and clearly. Faculty and others who have been skeptical in the past seem to like this new initiative. And I wonder why!

Maybe it's because much of the focus has been on improving management processes and eliminating bureaucratic red tape. Perhaps it's because the goal has been to involve more people, at all levels, in the decision-making processes. Or, it could be that our coeducators have always questioned those bothersome procedures and practices which were often without much substance.

In any event, I am more convinced than ever that the quality improvement thrust has been FVTC's greatest initiative since it began in 1967. I sense a new air of excitement reverberating through the halls! I see smiling staff at all levels, and I detect increased customer-first emphasis in service departments, classrooms, laboratories, and shops.

This book about quality describes the transformation that is occurring at FVTC. It explains the quality improvement model, unique to education, that evolved at the college from the theories and plans of famous quality gurus. It details new organizational structures, employee-centered management roles, and new initiatives that have emerged during this transformation. Most of all, it presents evidence that the quality process produces results in both customer satisfaction and reduction of costs, while improving the environment of the school and the quality of instruction and service.

As this innovative process goes perpetually onward, there will surely be some advances and some setbacks. But our abbreviated experience causes me to say without hesitation:

- Techniques and processes of quality and productivity can be transplanted successfully to education.

- Models from business and industry can be used in the design of curriculum and the scheduling and delivery of instruction.

- Quality processes can improve the management and operation of educational institutions while improving the learning environment and student achievement.

ACKNOWLEDGMENTS

I am thankful for the privilege to associate with all those who have been a part of the FVTC story. I am especially grateful for the opportunity to be a part of the original administrative team of the college, including my predecessor, William Sirek, and his deputy director, Dominic Bordini. Equally valued is my association with the other esteemed colleagues who made up my first executive cabinet: Donald Beno, Merlin Gentz, Robert Martin, Kathleen Paris, and Jerry Rickman.

Most of all, I am appreciative of my association and friendship with the outstanding faculty and staff who have made FVTC what it is today. Their loyalty and dedication to our cause and their unwavering devotion to their students is a story in itself. Many of these kind people have contributed to my education in the subject of quality and productivity in education. They have tolerated the many initiatives that accompanied my tenure as an administrator at the college. All have exhibited excellence in their day-to-day activities.

I owe the Quality Academy staff my deep appreciation for their willingness to carry the quality in education message to our staff, to businesses in our region, and to other educators around the world. That team and many other people have contributed to my knowledge on this subject.

This book could never have been completed without the dedicated skill and perseverance of my executive assistant, Jo Hillman. She has assisted me for over 20 years and has always been the perfect role model for displaying quality in her professional pursuits. I marvel at her creativity as she teaches customer service and other workshops about quality to our staff and others. Her editorial work has helped make this book more readable and grammatically correct.

I am grateful to Debby DeRosso for word processing. The entire Information Processing staff deserves recognition for their help and, in particular, Amy Schiedermayer for her expertise and skill in processing most of the copy.

Several other people contributed to this book and assisted me in developing my commitment to quality in education. Some are named below, but many are not listed.

Editorial Review –   Mary Lee Rudnick-Kaun,

Carol Tyler, Callie Zilinsky,

Terri Langan, Don Sleeger,

Jeanne Joseph, and Alice Strauss

Graphic Artwork –   Mary Ehman

Research Assistance –   Carol Mishler, Janet Perry

Retreat Team –   Carol Tyler, Don Sleeger,

Bob Martin, Merlin Gentz,

Jerry Rickman, Jo Hillman,

Mary Lee Rudnick-Kaun, Dan Ost,

Carol Mishler, Judy Arndt,

Fran Henry, and Diana Van Asten

To all who have helped me over the years, my sincere thanks.

Stan Spanbauer
1992

INTRODUCTION

Enhancing human resources through education has become a national priority. Following a decade or so of critical reports and recommended reforms, education has entered the political arena with full force. President Bush has been hailed as the "Education President," and governors and legislators around the country are trying new programs to turn the tide of complaints about our "failing educational system." These politicians have come to realize what educators have been saying for years, "People, not machines, will be the driving force behind our country's economic growth." For even though the private sector spends more money on training and development, our public educational system is capable, I believe, of becoming the primary force that impacts increasing productivity in our economy.

Critics of education abound. Somber reports show that positive change has not occurred despite numerous attempts at reform. These reports show the following defects that exist in American education:

- Per-pupil spending was 33 percent more in 1991 than in 1981 while student achievement (based on scholastic achievement scores) remained stagnant.

- The gulf in per-pupil spending between the wealthiest and poorest schools in our country is the widest in the past 20 years, sometimes reaching as much as $3,000 per pupil from one district to another.

- Many students who start college are not prepared for entry-level classes. Nearly 60 percent of today's 17-year-olds lack the reading skills needed to comprehend materials in higher education.

- The average level of skill attainment in education does not match the work force skill requirements of the future, causing business and industry to spend millions on basic skills educational programs for their employees.

- Secondary public school dropout rates continue to average about 30 percent and exceed 50 percent in most of the larger cities of the United States. The dropout rate for minorities approaches 70 percent in urban centers. As a result, over a million students disappear from education each year.

- Scholastic Achievement Test (SAT) scores for 1991 hit an all-time low in verbal skills testing with mathematics scores declining for the first time since 1980.

- About 20 percent of United States adults are functionally illiterate.

- American students test two to three years behind their French, German, and Japanese counterparts in both math and science examinations at the high school level.[1]

At the same time, some people contend that schools are constantly improving, always responding to the needs of the community. Mostly, educators claim that while public schools are the most responsive of our institutions, expectations for schools are changing faster than the schools can possibly respond. These people maintain that our nation is asking too much of schools. How can they expect to solve economic crises overnight when the problems have been festering and intensifying for several decades?

One thing is clear. No matter how good our schools are, or how good they have been, schools must be even better in the future to meet the needs of a rapidly changing world. Educators must be committed to creating a climate in which excellence can thrive. Such a climate is evidenced by these conditions:

- A commitment to helping students succeed to the very best of their ability, with vast improvement in retention rates and college entrance exam scores.

- Awareness that school management must change and incorporate many of the organizational reforms common in business and industry.

- Recognition that teachers play major roles in quality and productivity initiatives while assuming greater roles in school management functions.

- Development and enhancement of learning theory which assures that students are mastering needed knowledge and skills.

- Establishment of educational standards that ensure that every student leaves school with demonstrated abilities to read, write, compute, and perform at levels comparable to other countries.

- Demonstration of a new spirit of caring for students, taxpayers, and fellow educators.

- Communication with students and citizens that is vastly improved so that there is a connection between a high-quality education and the hopes we have for our future and country.

- Recognition that a well-educated work force is basic to a solid economy and necessary to maintain a competitive edge among other countries.

- Guarantee that students leave school with labor-market readiness and mastery of skills necessary for high productivity, including the capacity to learn, think, work effectively, and solve problems.

- Collaboration with business, industry, and the community, since their help and support is crucial to the success of our endeavors.

- Focus on the processes which have created hassles and bureaucracies rather than on people who are involved.

- Use of quality/productivity techniques which are helping U.S. business and industry regain their competitive edge with foreign competition.[2]

The problems of education in the United States are not just school system problems. They are diverse, deep-rooted, and as much social and political as they are educational. However, educational failures can be explained in part by the way today's schools are structured and managed. These labor-intensive institutions operate much the same as they did more than a century ago. Fundamental causes of poor academic performance are not found in the schools but rather in the institutions that have traditionally governed the schools. I believe that how much students learn is not determined only by their aptitude or family background, but also by how effectively schools are organized. The key to better schools, therefore, is in institutional reform in which the productive potential already present in schools is harnessed. It rests in granting educators the autonomy to do what they do best.

This restructuring of American education is needed because economic growth, competitiveness, and living standards directly correlate with the state of our schools. The outmoded system and discredited practices of most American schools need fundamental changes to provide an environment that fosters creativity and greater participation by those most affected, the students and their teachers. We need cultural change from the top down and away from the authoritarian management and bureaucratic practices that have been a part of our educational system for years.

The rebuilding of American schools requires a model that examines each and every management and teaching process in order to promote continued and permanent reform. Radical change is needed to eliminate the cumbersome systems that exist in many schools today. The reformation of American education demands a model for quality improvement with proven success, similar to those tested and practiced in business and industry. It requires a long-term comprehensive approach rather than piecemeal approaches to deal with problems.[3]

My first book on this topic, *Quality First in Education...Why Not?*, outlined reasons *why* this type of long-range reform was needed in schools. This book tells *how* it can be done, emphasizing that the quality first improvement process will be slow, but steady; continuous, and permanent. Both books stress that the quality model advocated is not the panacea for the ills of education. Rather, the model encourages educators to carefully define improvement needs and requirements in advance in order to bring about a meaningful change in education.

This model is based on the belief that major improvements in quality and productivity can be made in schools, just as they have in manufacturing and service companies. It was designed on the premise that the public is receptive to business community and school system partnerships, and that the current educational climate is ready for the improvements that business and industry have to offer. These private sector changes require four major improvement features for schools:

1. Management and teaching philosophies that focus on defined measures of excellence and quality improvement.

2. Goals that meet or exceed the expectations of internal and external customers (students, employees, taxpayers, and employers).

3. Customer satisfaction systems and organizational climates that prevent errors and eliminate defects.

4. Decisions based on input from those closest to the students, using data obtained from research, not guesswork or hunches.

I believe that schools can improve through carefully controlled changes in management. It's possible for schools to make steady progress toward defined goals through the preparation of, and adherence to, agreed-upon process design with stated conforming requirements. It's also possible to create changes in student and teacher attitudes while effecting reductions in costs. This new accountability system calls for all teachers, administrators, and support staff to be involved in the management of schools. It requires restructured schools, with new roles and new responsibilities. With these changes comes a new accountability for performance, with standards clear to all.

These improvement efforts may initially cause apprehension and tension in those involved. They may cause misunderstandings among parents, students, teachers, board members, and employers who hire graduates. And because the changes are gradual, the slow progress may dampen the motivation of those involved who want quick results.

While steady improvement will soon become apparent, those involved will quickly realize that the quest for quality improvement must continue perpetually. The alternative, moving from crisis to crisis in a constant search for reform, is no longer acceptable. A systematic approach to improving quality is the only solution. Use of this model will result in a planned approach to make our schools better places to learn and to work.

CHAPTER 1

THE BEGINNING

In 1985, a two-year technical college in northeastern Wisconsin began using quality processes in both its management and instruction. School officials, aware of the cry for reform in education throughout the country, decided to examine these three questions.

- Can the techniques and processes of quality and productivity be transplanted successfully from the private sector to public higher education?

- Is it possible to use industrial models in the design of curriculum and in the scheduling and delivery of instruction at the post-secondary level?

- Can quality processes used in the business world to increase productivity be used to improve the management and operation of schools?

This chapter describes the early stages of implementation of the quality process at FVTC.

Near the end of a rather routine planning meeting involving college staff and several chief executive officers from the Fox Valley region, Frank Koffend, president of Akrosil, Inc., made a parting suggestion, "Why don't you look into offering training at your school in zero defects management?" I asked him what "zero defects management" was, and he explained that it was a term for incorporating quality improvement processes in an organization to totally eliminate errors, thereby improving services to customers.

In a few days, I received a copy of Philip B. Crosby's book *Quality Is Free* with a letter from Frank encouraging me to read it. His letter prompted me to meet with a group of our management instructors to talk about quality and productivity training. They informed me that they were teaching the basic concepts of quality in our Supervisory Management Program. They had heard of Crosby, but they were more familiar with other quality experts such as W. Edwards Deming, Joseph Juran, Karl Albrecht, and Glenn E. Hayes.

My interest was piqued when they said that a number of companies in our region were beginning to implement quality improvement processes in their production and internal operations. I formed a committee of individuals from different departments of the college and asked them to conduct a study about quality improvement processes. One committee member was my executive assistant, Jo Hillman, who became intently interested in the topic. As a participant in the Wisconsin Technical College Leadership Identification Program, she conducted a year long study to examine quality and productivity applications in business and industry. The expertise she gained on the subject later proved to be invaluable.

The state office of Vocational/Technical Education in Wisconsin also became involved during 1985 when they gave our college a small grant to design an overview quality and productivity curriculum for possible statewide use. This effort was coordinated by Bill Ihlenfeldt, then manager of economic development at the college, and copies of the curriculum were subsequently distributed to the other technical colleges in Wisconsin.

I began to notice magazine and newspaper articles on the topics of quality and productivity. All seemed to say the same thing: The initiation of quality processes in an organization can have a significant, positive impact, including better working conditions, improved services, and increased profits. It became obvious that the quality movement was a major thrust in the world of business and industry.

In the meantime, our task force on quality reported their findings. They had visited numerous companies in the region that were engaged in quality improvement programs and they had also read several books and articles on the subject. Their report and the study by Hillman supported my belief that the quality movement was gaining momentum in the United States and in our region. The team unanimously recommended that our college begin to design and teach formal programs in quality and productivity for business and industry.

The decision to start formal training in quality came easily, but committing to implement these private sector concepts into college operations was more difficult. Before the decision was made, there were numerous discussions with other school administrators and continued conversations with individuals in the private sector such as Koffend. He was pleased that we decided to design training programs in quality, but wondered aloud whether FVTC had the expertise to do it. After all, his company had invested a lot of money obtaining training materials, instruction, and consulting services from a nationally-known consulting firm. Another skeptic was Lee Erickson, then a FVTC board member and manager of employee relations at Thilmany Pulp and Paper Company. He shared Koffend's concern that we were getting into training that we knew little about. And they were right!

These concerns were weighed when the college decided to implement quality improvement processes. I have always felt that our college should serve as a model to the business world in all services in which we offer instruction. Examples are our food service, data processing, child care, and information processing departments. These departments serve as models of excellence for similar businesses throughout our region. Based on that philosophy, I decided to select an industry model, adapt it to education, and use it as an operational plan for our school. I hoped that we would gain greater credibility in the private sector by adopting their ideas about quality improvement.

In August 1986, I approached the board with a proposal to begin the training which would lead to the implementation of a formal quality improvement process at FVTC. I asked for a three-year budget of $60,000 and provided a list of long-range goals for the 1985-90 period. These goals, outlined in Appendix A, included broad targets related to improvement of overall organizational climate, customer services, and the initiation of "guaranteed" customer satisfaction. To my surprise, there were only a few questions after my presentation, and the board endorsed the initiative. Our journey in quality had begun!

Arrangements were then made for a board member and me to attend the Executive College at Philip B. Crosby Associates in Winter Park, Florida. We decided to associate with Crosby primarily because our mentor company, Akrosil, Inc., had worked with them and also because the Crosby model seemed best suited for a service-type institution. The Deming approach seemed too statistically-oriented for us and Juran appeared to focus too much on quality control, rather than prevention. An in-depth review of those models and other prevalent ones shows that many components and concepts are the same—many elements are common to all models. Gloria Pursell, then dean of community relations at FVTC, prepared a chart showing the common elements of quality (see Table 1.1).

	Philip Crosby	W. Edwards Deming	Joseph Juran	Karl Albrecht Ron Zemke	Glenn E. Hayes
Clear Mission	X	X	X	X	X
Teamwork	X	X	X	X	X
New Culture	X	X	X	X	X
Customer First	X	X	X	X	X
Define Quality	X	X	X	X	X
Education	X	X	X	X	X
Measurement	X	X	X	X	X
Everyone's Responsibility	X	X	X	X	X

Table 1.1 – Common Elements of Quality

The Executive College workshop was excellent. The training was exceptional and the customer service and internal operations were letter-perfect. It was obvious to both Lee Erickson, my board member companion, and me that the management consulting firm practiced what it preached. The training modules were highly structured and the instructors had extensive experience in implementing quality and productivity processes. We were given the basics of quality and were provided with the rationale for getting involved. Most of all, the instructors stressed the need for top-level commitment. It was obvious that the CEO and other top executives needed a passion for quality improvement.

I sketched a preliminary FVTC Plan for Quality during our return flight to Wisconsin. I was convinced that quality and productivity concepts could be successfully used in education. I was sure that our faculty and staff would accept the idea because they had always been willing to try new initiatives. After all, didn't they cooperate in converting the college to an institution that uses a competency-based curricula and a system of continuous enrollment and graduation of students? Don't they use media, computers, and other technology to enhance education and individualized instruction? Hasn't this school received several national awards? Wouldn't this be another project to add to the list of innovations that have become a way of life at FVTC?

I wasn't fully prepared for what was to come! I soon learned that we were getting involved in the most significant and challenging undertaking I had been associated with during my 20+ years in education. It became apparent that we had embarked on something that would ultimately permeate every single activity in our college. We had begun a journey of hard work that ultimately unfolded into intermittent patterns of frustration, joy, success, failure, change, and progress. During those early days, I often wondered if it was worth the effort and the anxiety. It is.

When we started the formal quality first process, we used the Crosby model as our implementation strategy. We soon decided that it wasn't sufficient for education so we designed our own model. The FVTC model is a 16-step strategy that includes the best of approaches by quality experts, including Crosby, Deming, Albrecht, and Juran. Our model is summarized in Appendix B.

The quality journey we began in 1985 began to influence many of our major decisions. As more staff were trained, a new, common language emerged. A new excitement prevailed throughout the school. We had always had a common goal—to be the best technical school anywhere. I knew that we finally had the strategy to make it happen!

CHAPTER 2

COMMITMENT FROM THE TOP

When implementing quality and productivity improvement on a school-wide basis, top management needs to play a major role in promoting the process and making appropriate changes in policies, procedures, and systems.

This top-level commitment is essential to show everyone that executives and board members solidly support the quality improvement process. Since senior administrators make decisions strongly influencing quality improvement techniques, their commitment must be assured first. They ultimately serve as role models and are responsible for creating and maintaining an environment that fosters the quality improvement process.

CEO Commitment

The CEO's most important job is to create a vision and sense of purpose for the organization. Creating that vision involves imagining possible achievements and detailing action plans to get there. According to Patterson, Purkey, and Parker, educational leaders can take five steps to move vision into action.

1. Valuing—Leaders see the vision

2. Reflection—Leaders accept the vision

3. Articulation—Leaders make their vision public

4. Planning—Leaders develop strategies

5. Action—Leaders mobilize people[4]

Unless the chief school officer leads the way, the concept is doomed to failure. Middle-level managers alone cannot ensure success. The school head must demonstrate strong and sustained commitment and lead the way while encouraging principals, vice principals, and other supervisors to take the effort seriously. This commitment will create a favorable environment which will help others to persevere in their efforts to incorporate the quality improvement process into regular routines and procedures.

The top person oversees the total system, including school programs, personnel, and finances. He or she knows the internal political environment and can ensure that adequate planning and coordination activities are targeted for constant improvement. The chief executive leads the effort to build trust within the school system. While this trust ultimately hinges on past performances, frequent contact and strong personal skills help the chief develop good relationships with staff and community. But telling people to do it is not enough. Only when the CEO perpetually demonstrates the attitudes, communications, and support for all levels will acceptance come from the ranks. The CEO helps people strive to do the job right the first time through positive encouragement, coaching, and mentoring.

The CEO is mainly responsible for establishing the plan and strategy for the school's future. Too often these are short-term and unorderly— there is no comprehensive plan. The quality process demands an orderly, long-term framework for planning which ensures continued improvement.

When the plan for quality improvement is implemented, the CEO controls the resources to help make it successful. The CEO can ensure that the right personnel are selected and that school communications systems support the process. He or she can ensure continued monitoring of the new systems. Through this top-level direction, quality elements (Standards of Excellence) are determined for the school and conforming requirements are written and tested.

Since the model encourages greater involvement of all staff and shared decision making, the CEO should also encourage new management strategies that are based on greater collaboration and shared leadership. He or she promotes the empowerment of teachers. Conditions and structures are created to encourage teachers and staff to explore new systems in an atmosphere that encourages innovation. The CEO must advocate a system that is less hierarchical and more integrated. The promotion of a "flattened" organization and the formulation of objectives to support this direction are signs of commitment at the top.

Once the quality process plan is in place, the school head must communicate the new vision and convince and motivate those most affected—the internal and external customers. Since the CEO is the quality improvement process salesperson for the college, special communication skills are required. The school chief must constantly demonstrate quality to everyone with whom he or she comes in contact. If the top administrator of the school remains office-bound and autocratic, a quality improvement process will be difficult to implement.

In the end, having and communicating a quality process plan is not enough. The CEO must also make sure that the process gets underway, builds momentum, and continues to move forward. To make the process deep-rooted, the CEO identifies key people, delegates responsibilities, and provides the leadership skills required to cause the transformation. The chief administrator continually supports people at all levels to keep the process perpetually growing.[5]

Board Commitment

It is also essential that school board members develop and sustain commitment to the quality improvement process. Since the board establishes school policy and approves school budgets, members must receive a strong orientation to enlist their continued support for its implementation and continuation.

One way to make this happen is to find board "champions" for the movement. Once these supporters are identified, the CEO begins the motivational thrust to foster continued growth and endorsement by the board.

Commitment cannot stop after the policies are in place and the quality movement is started. Board members should require evidence that quality elements are established and conforming requirements are detailed and measured. The school quality coordinator should report regularly at board meetings to keep members informed. The coordinator should also present an annual report on quality to the board and then distribute copies to all employees.

Total Quality Leadership Council

A steering committee also exhibits commitment. At FVTC, this steering committee, the Total Quality Leadership Council (TQLC), is the planning group and focal point for activity for the quality process.

The steering committee meets regularly and circulates minutes of the proceedings to all school employees. All levels of personnel are represented on the committee so the various school groups recognize the importance of their participation. The quality coordinator prepares the agenda, conducts the meeting, and controls the overall operation of the council.

The school CEO remains a permanent member of the council by attending meetings regularly and participating actively with the other members. Other top school administrators should participate on other quality and productivity committees as well. This sends an important message about commitment to school employees.

Quality Policies

According to Juran, quality policies "are prepared to provide guidelines for (1) planning the overall quality program and (2) defining the action to be taken in situations for which personnel have requested guidance."[6] He insists that no single set of quality policies can fit all activities and suggests the creation of several levels of quality policies throughout the organization.

The board adopts the initial quality policy which becomes the guide for action in the school district. The quality policy confirms the board's commitment and declares to all that quality is paramount. The policy provides the overall framework for administrative and departmental procedures in the school.

Since policies are statements of belief upon which procedures are built, the quality policy should be clear and useful enough to be accepted throughout the school. Once adopted, quality policies must be communicated across the organization. One way is to include policy statements on all important school documents, such as the strategic plan, the budget, and other similar reports.

The most common form of quality policy is a brief statement of philosophy. Figure 2.1 shows the FVTC Quality First Policy. It identifies the school's internal and external customers and provides a statement of intent to meet their needs.

FVTC Quality First Policy

It is the policy of Fox Valley Technical College to provide quality instruction and service consistent with the highest educational standards. We endeavor to provide precise, prompt, and courteous service and instruction to our students, to one another, and to the employers who hire our graduates and use our services.

Figure 2.1 – FVTC Policy on Quality First

As the quality movement grows, additional board policies may be adopted, such as the one shown in Figure 2.2. This "Guarantee for Contracted Services" assures satisfaction of customized training and technical assistance programs conducted for business and industry. Another board policy found in Figure 2.3 relates to placement of FVTC graduates. This "Guaranteed Retraining Policy" gives graduates who are unable to find employment in occupations related to their original field of study continued opportunities to be successful in the job market through more education and services provided at no additional cost. These types of guarantees show that quality is important and that customers' needs are top priority.

Besides establishing policies, the board of education should provide the financial resources to start and continue the quality process. Since consultant costs are generally high and training materials are expensive, up-front costs may be substantial. In a school district of 1,000 students, for example, it is estimated that an annual budget of approximately $20,000 will be needed.

After the first few years, the costs for quality training are reduced. Future years' costs are estimated in Chapter 8, "Statistical Approaches to Measuring and Costing Quality in Education." Approximately 1 percent of the total school budget should be allocated to support the quality process. Funds are needed for training, committee work, quality commitment days, newsletters, and salaries for those associated directly with quality process improvement. Once the process is fully underway, the school's investment will be offset by improved service and instruction and reduced operating costs.

Guarantee for Contracted Services

POLICY

If a customer (company, organization, or individual) is dissatisfied with the customized training (instruction) of contracted services, the customer is entitled to have the appropriate portion of the customized training redone at no additional charge.

DEFINITIONS

Contracted Services Consultant	Person authorized to develop service contracts for the district.
Customer	Business, industry, organization, individual, or group which requests contracted customized training or technical assistance.
Contracted Service	Courses or services which currently exist or are developed or modified to meet the specific service needs of an employer. The courses or services may be offered "in plant," at FVTC, or in another facility.
Technical Assistance	Consultation or services other than instruction which are offered to individuals or businesses.

Figure 2.2 – Guarantee for Business and Industry Training

Guaranteed Retraining Policy

Fox Valley Technical College graduates of programs at least one year in length who do not obtain employment in their program or related area within six months of graduation are guaranteed up to **six free credits** of additional instruction PLUS other student services.

Figure 2.3 – Guaranteed Placement Job Readiness Policy

Integration

A final way to demonstrate commitment is to ensure that quality improvement becomes integrated into everyday practices and functions of the school. Administrators, managers, and committee chairs should give regular reports pertaining to quality. Research reports and other information about quality should be disseminated throughout the school. All staff should be continually encouraged to incorporate quality in everyday operations and functions.

Some Reflections And Thoughts On Application

At first I thought that commitment to the quality improvement process would be easy. Since I was in "control" of personnel and resources, all I needed to do, I thought, was to point them toward the quality improvement process. I didn't realize that I would be specifically targeted to be a visible exhibitor of quality.

Being in the "quality fishbowl" requires a continuous examination of everything I do. It's been a humbling experience to realize that many quality problems in the school are really the direct result of my actions. Five years into the process, I am still in the fishbowl and am constantly reminded about the "quality" way to do things.

From early on, the Fox Valley Technical College Board was very supportive of the quality improvement process. I had two members who were quality champions and I regularly called on them to support the movement. One served on one of our quality committees and the other gave several presentations on quality to various groups. Support wavered only slightly when one board member called for evidence that the process was reducing costs. There was initial difficulty in providing actual data to show direct relationships of cost reduction to the quality process, and the dissenting member began to question continuation of the process. The other eight board members continued to give solid support to the quality improvement process.

I learned that it's essential that board members be updated continually about quality. I invite them to every function related to quality, especially those programs and activities that include people from the business community. Usually, I can count on business people to support our effort and encourage our movement.

The board policy on quality was developed very early in the process. The executive cabinet and I looked at several examples of business and industry policies, one was written and revised by our Total Quality Leadership Council, and taken to the board for action. It was passed without much discussion. After that, I did whatever possible to make the policy visible. I asked our marketing staff to include it in every major publication. Copies were printed and circulated to all management staff. Wooden plaques that carried the policy were prepared and given to all members of our administrative council to display in their offices.

The Total Quality Leadership Council (TQLC) was formed very early in the process. The first council consisted of the senior executives of the college. One of our first actions was to select the college's first quality coordinator. We reviewed the credentials of several people in the organization and decided that the first coordinator should be someone who exhibited quality routinely in everyday professional life. We wanted someone who would be an excellent teacher and would also be a role model.

Our first quality coordinator, Gloria Pursell, was appointed in 1986. She was an excellent choice. She and the rest of the TQLC received training from our consultant during the first year.

Following her initial training, Gloria began to plan and conduct the TQLC meetings. She established the agenda, ran the meetings, and prepared minutes. She reported directly to me and this made it apparent to our staff that this was an important position.

The first TQLC established the framework for the quality improvement process at FVTC. The group decided on the training plan for the rest of the managers and approved the guidelines for the council's operation.

Gradually, new members were added to the TQLC. At first, they were all top-management staff, but after some time, all levels of personnel were included. As time went on, the council became more action-oriented. I was an active member but tried not to dominate the meetings. While it was difficult at first to give up control, the council became very effective, and I felt good about that.

Another way I demonstrated commitment to quality was to include the topic as an agenda item at every administrative council meeting. As the primary decision-making body of the college, the council approves administrative policies and suggests most new board policies. The quality coordinator became a regular member and she gave a report at each council meeting. The merging of the TQLC and the administrative council will further integrate the quality movement with everyday operations and governance.

During its first year, the TQLC developed a budget for quality. A separate budget account was established and the quality coordinator was given responsibility for its use. The early budgets were difficult to determine since most items were not integrated into regular school functions. As the quality process matured, more integration occurred, linking regular college activities to the process.

My commitment continues to be absolutely essential to the success of the quality improvement movement. Without active and unwavering support by the top administrators and me, the whole process may break down. With that realization, it has become one of the most important functions of my position. I personally see that there is a constant review of everything that occurs to ensure that our quality process becomes a way of life.

Commitment means much more than giving an annual speech on how important quality is to our school. It requires unending enthusiasm and devotion to quality improvement. It calls for an almost fanatic promotion of and attention to new ways to do things. It requires constant review of each and every action.

Summary

The school's chief administrator is the mentor and leader in the quality/productivity movement in the school. Through his or her efforts, the process starts, continues, and flourishes. Since there are ups and downs, the CEO must continually renew efforts to reinforce the processes' significance to everyone in the school.

The CEO establishes a new management style based on greater collaboration and shared leadership with the faculty and staff. He or she ensures that the system becomes less hierarchical and more integrated and that there are fewer layers between the customer and top management. The CEO initiates the movement to promote teacher and staff empowerment through an atmosphere that fosters shared decision making and innovation.

It is also necessary for the board to demonstrate commitment to and support for the quality process. Establishing quality policies for the school sets the stage for new administrative policies and procedures that enhance the process. Through solid orientation and training, board members will become champions for quality in both the college and communities they represent.

The quality process requires allocation of personnel and financial resources to support it. The CEO ensures that there is an adequate budget to meet the costs for training and other quality efforts. As productivity is improved, the initial investment provides a payback to the school in the form of improved services and instruction and reduced operating costs.

The CEO makes sure that the TQLC is organized and operational. A quality coordinator is named to coordinate the process in the organization, and rotation plans are established to provide opportunities for more people to participate in quality activities.

In short, the CEO and other top executives of the school district must become the visible champions for quality. They must walk and talk quality and understand that change happens by degree, not by decree. When supporting change and reformation of schools to enhance quality improvement, senior executives help the transformation move along on a steady journey toward the ultimate goal of total quality.

CHAPTER 3

EDUCATION AND TRAINING

To ensure constant awareness and to promote understanding of each individual's role in keeping the quality concept going, a strong staff education program is required. This program provides staff with the techniques and skills to perform their jobs using quality improvement processes. During this training, faculty and service department workers learn the necessary concepts and techniques to help eliminate poor quality practices and reduce costs that occur because of defects or errors.

A model should be selected for use during the training. There are several that are available throughout the country, including those advocated by Deming, Crosby, and Juran. When examining various models, it will soon be obvious that they have several common elements or process steps. Because of this, most experts concur that any model can be used when the process starts. Most organizations begin with one model and then, as the implementation moves forward, they design their own. FVTC originally used the Crosby 14-step model and then designed its own 16-step plan. The 16-step plan is shown in Appendix B.

The recommended educational plan calls for a top-down strategy with chief administrators and board members receiving an initial 20-hour executive training program. This provides an orientation to the quality improvement process and creates an understanding of the role that senior management plays. Board members learn about their role as policymakers for the school.

The initial training of top executives and board members should be conducted off-site by a consulting firm. Several excellent executive workshops in quality processes are available. Some are specific to education, including those available from Delaware Community College in Philadelphia, Pennsylvania, and Lakeshore Technical College in Cleveland, Wisconsin. The Academy for Quality in Education, located at FVTC, also has workshops for school board members and executives.

The second phase of education and training is geared for middle managers such as principals, vice principals, coordinators, supervisors, and managers. School union officials also should be invited to participate in these middle-management workshops since they will play key roles in the successful initiation of the quality improvement process.

During these workshops, the quality process model is studied and the specific role of managers is clearly defined. Since the middle manager's function is critical to the implementation of the quality process, the role is detailed, studied, and practiced by the managers. Each manager learns to articulate his or her role in the process and use the skills acquired to become the quality coach and teacher in his or her department.

Faculty are the largest group involved in quality improvement education and their training should be completed early in the process. In these sessions, faculty learn the basic concepts of quality improvement and are introduced to a common language of quality. The role of the instructor is outlined in the elements for curriculum and instruction which are reviewed and debated.

The introductory course for instructors at FVTC was designed by a group of teachers selected as being exemplary by their peers and managers. The course was taught by faculty who were selected following intensive interviews. This introductory course did not cover the complex issues related to teacher roles, participatory management, or differentiated staffing. However, it did make faculty aware of possible new roles and new ways to operate schools. It gave them a good orientation to quality in education and prepared them for further involvement.

Typically, teachers' roles have been identified with actual contact with students and their work loads calculated exclusively by hours of contact. However, as teachers assume new leadership roles in the quality-based school, their positions will be looked on in a different light. In this new environment, teachers will become managers of learning processes; and advisers, counselors, planners, curriculum specialists, and school representatives in the business community.

It is necessary, therefore, to define these roles for faculty based on these new responsibilities. They are identified in the quality elements related to curriculum and instruction, and conforming requirements are detailed to serve as the criteria. As new roles emerge and as school organizational structures become less hierarchical, new titles and updated systems which challenge tradition will emerge.

An educational program should also be planned for service department staff. These people should receive an orientation to the new concepts and learn the basic principles and common language of quality. Applications of the quality improvement process to the various service departments should be discussed, debated, and practiced.

A structured orientation course should be made available for new faculty and staff, as well as new board members. This training should be conducted as soon as possible so new staff and board members learn to appreciate the importance of the quality initiative to the school district.

This initial education and training is vital to the success of the quality improvement process. Through these programs, all people in the organization receive a thorough introduction to quality and learn about its application to education.

The initial FVTC Education and Training Plan is found in Figure 3.1. The top-down sequence was emphasized in Phase I training. Following the first phase of orientation and training, specialized courses were provided for the various personnel levels in schools.

This second phase of training for managers, teachers, and service staff enabled them to learn more about their specific roles in the process. All groups received training in communication skills, problem-solving techniques, customer service, and team building methods. They were introduced to measurement, charting, and costing processes and, through practical application, began to apply statistical analysis and use control systems. Phase II training is specific to the personnel level of the group and meaningful to each individual.

Phase II of the FVTC Training and Education Plan is shown in Figure 3.2. These courses were planned with the assistance of a peer committee, and pilot courses were conducted before the mass training began. In addition to these staff training programs, a training program for student workers was also initiated. This program places major focus on customer service.

Education and training is an ongoing activity in the quality-based school. Managers, instructors, counselors, technical staff, and service workers should be given continued opportunities to participate in workshops, seminars, and courses related to quality. An important role of the quality coordinator is to alert school personnel about upcoming professional development activities on quality and to encourage people to participate.

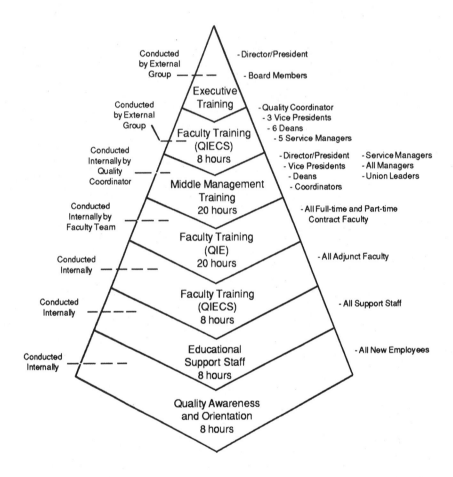

Figure 3.1 – FVTC Phase I Training Plan

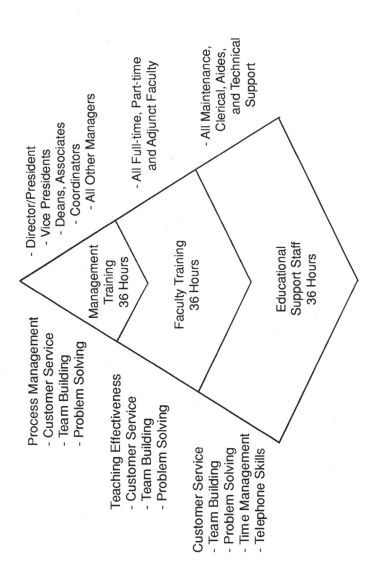

Figure 3.2 – FVTC Phase II Training Plan

Education And Training Committee

An education and training committee should be formed to develop a formal plan of education for the school and to facilitate its implementation. Committee members should be chosen from each employment level of the school. Their primary functions are:

1. To establish and monitor a yearly educational plan for the school.

2. To review existing training programs and make recommendations for modification.

3. To assist the other committees in the selection of programs and speakers for inservice and quality process celebration events.

The education and training plan seeks to enhance professional competence for teachers, managers, and service workers in both their defined position description and in new skills related to quality. Employees throughout the organization look to the future and prepare for change through a sequence of planned activities, all related to professional development. In this process, staff develop special skills to improve:

- Relationships with self and family
- Relationships with students
- Relationships with co-workers
- Relationships with those in the community

This model of integrated relationships developed at FVTC during Phase I development is shown in Figure 3.3. It forms the basis for improved teaching and learning processes through better relationships.

The ultimate goal of the education and training committee is to integrate training specific to quality with all other professional development activities of both the school and the individual. Everyone in the school should have a written professional development plan linked with performance reviews and the conforming requirements which are identified in the quality elements. This individual plan integrates professional goals with individual career aspirations.

Some Reflections And Thoughts On Application

The education and training plan that we designed at FVTC has been successful. I don't believe I'd change any part of it with the possible exception of providing more intensive training for middle managers during the early stages.

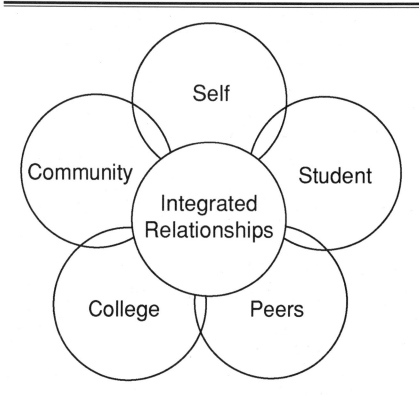

Figure 3.3 – FVTC Model of Integrated Relationships

Perhaps the best part of the plan was the course designed specifically for instructors. The course laid the foundation for faculty acceptance of the quality process. The idea to use faculty to teach other instructors was a superb concept that originated from course designers Carol Tyler and Callie Zilinsky, and our second quality coordinator, Jeanne Joseph. The workshop presenters became very knowledgeable about quality concepts and techniques. What better way to reinforce quality among several key faculty than to ask them to teach the system to their coeducators?

I also think it was a good idea to mandate participation by all full-time faculty, managers, and service department workers. At first, I wondered what we would do if someone refused to participate. After all, we were asking them to attend these classes at times which were often beyond their contract hours. To my amazement, all employees attended the classes regularly and most seemed to enjoy the experience. Those who conducted the training had tough standards, including strict attendance requirements. If someone missed a session, they were required to make up the work. Grades were withheld if any work was not made up. No one complained; acceptance of the training was universal.

The workshop evaluations were very positive. The vast majority enjoyed the opportunity to learn about quality processes and to have the chance to discuss ways to make things better. Figure 3.4 is a composite of the numerical evaluations that were tabulated for the Phase I training of adjunct staff. They are representative of the kinds of positive evaluations received from all the groups.

424 Responses

A = Strongly Agree
B = Agree
C = Disagree
D = Strongly Disagree

1. Course objectives and/or processes are provided and met.

"A" 178   "B" 241   "C" 5

2. This course is adding to my understanding of quality at FVTC.

"A" 214   "B" 196   "C" 12   "D" 2

3. Overall, I would rate the training I am receiving as:

Excellent - 180   Good - 213   Fair - 27   Poor - 4

Figure 3.4 – Quality Phase I Training Evaluation (QIECS)

Some incentives were built into the training plan. Wherever possible, faculty and staff were given the opportunity to attend classes during their regularly assigned hours. The courses were approved for meeting certification requirements for faculty and managers. In some cases, credit was given for advancement on the salary schedule. Adjunct faculty were provided with a dinner and a small stipend for attending, since they were required to participate during their non-assigned hours.

The teachers who conducted the Phase I training became a self-directed team. They met regularly to share successes and challenges. They compared notes and made several changes in the curriculum, especially after the pilot classes. Whenever possible, senior executives of the college attended the teachers' work sessions and discussed concerns. However, the group managed itself and did a remarkable job! The success of this group led to formation of The Academy for Quality in Education.

The academy was established to design and teach quality process courses and workshops to educators from other schools. Because the idea of using quality concepts in schools was new, it received much attention on both a state and national level. The academy is an independent, self-managed team that operates as a separate, self-supporting cost center. Educators from all over the country (and several foreign countries) attend workshops, request consultation, and purchase quality process training materials from the academy.

As it matured, the academy became involved in the establishment of a full-time associate degree program in quality process management. Academy staff were responsible for writing the curriculum and organizing the full-time program that was piloted with a group of students from Central America and formally initiated in the college in January 1991.

As the college's reputation grew and as it received national recognition for implementing quality, area company executives took notice. Soon the academy was asked to provide all types of quality/productivity courses and workshops for area business, industry, and agencies. Before long, requests came from throughout Wisconsin and from other states.

Two other major functions of the academy came later. One was the establishment of the Quality and Productivity Resource Center (Q/PRC) and an accompanying Community Quality Network. Another academy responsibility is to coordinate the delivery of the internal education and training program. The integration of internal and external quality instruction is a perpetual major initiative.

The Q/PRC and Community Quality Network were immediate successes. Several companies and individuals became members of the Q/PRC and used its services and resources to enhance their programs. A number of these companies became "Beacons" by contributing $5,000 or more to the center. The Community Quality Network now provides monthly informational programs with average attendance around 100. It is also self-supporting.

FVTC continues to learn from others who are involved in quality. Our initial association with an outside consultant was an excellent start for us. We launched our process and later designed our own model and training program based on our needs and experiences. This resulted in the design of an exemplary quality training department. Our full-time programs, workshops, resource centers, and training staff have been enhanced as we moved along the perpetual journey of quality. The outcome of all this is increased credibility in the business world and an improved internal process. We can now provide better services while developing excellent relationships with industry, agencies, and other schools. A certain pride comes with being the first public school to implement formal private sector quality/productivity practices into instruction and operations. This pride is shared with all faculty and staff of the college. It would not have been accomplished without an intensive education and training program for our own people.

Summary

One of the most important requirements of the quality process is the design and implementation of the staff education program. The program begins with an orientation and awareness course for all employees. The long-range goal is the design of an individual professional growth plan for each individual.

The recommended education plan calls for a top-down strategy. The senior management of the school receives training first, and the rest of the faculty and staff are trained soon after.

This chapter describes the model for training and education at FVTC. Also shown is the Phase II training plan which began in the fall of 1990 to provide specialized training geared toward specific roles at the college.

This chapter explains the model for integrated relationships that was designed by the original instructional task force.

The chapter concludes with an explanation of the quality academy and its role in providing training in quality/productivity to other schools, to business and industry, and to FVTC staff. The Quality/Productivity Resource Center is described and its relationship to the Community Quality Network is defined.

CHAPTER 4

TEAMS IN SCHOOLS

Education in this country has been, for the most part, a history of various cycles of reform. Most reform movements, including those currently proposed, have had little effect on the teaching/learning process. Most of them do nothing more than expand, solidify, and entrench traditional school bureaucracy. After reviewing reform movements, a major conclusion is that lasting and significant changes in education will not occur unless teachers and other staff are directly and actively involved in the planning and development of desired changes.

Such involvement by the people closest to the customer (teacher to student, service worker to customer) is paramount to the success of quality improvement strategies. The FVTC process model, similar to most quality models, gives opportunities for all employees to participate in the quality improvement movement. The primary strategy advocated to achieve participation is the establishment of teams.

Teams are groups of people who work together toward common ends. They are the cornerstone of the quality process. The school in this process has to perform as a large team in activities that cross work units and departments. The institution thereby accepts ownership in the large goals or strategic directions. Beyond this, smaller teams are used to solve particular problems in departments and work units. Because team formation promotes shared responsibility, a diversity of talents, perspectives, and commitments occur. Working in and through teams requires special skills on the part of both the team members and those who are responsible for management.

Teams can best solve problems because they have the expertise and are closest to the unit of work itself. They solve problems by building consensus around issues. Since they are most often the ones affected, it is common sense to ask the employees to participate in the resolution of their own problems. Teams consist of a multitude of interests and opinions which need to be expressed before long-term elimination of problems and errors can occur.

In its simplest form, teamwork can be defined as joint action by a group of people in which each individual subordinates his or her interests and opinions to the unity and interests of the group. Therefore, teamwork, participation, and involvement are integral concepts. Teamwork reaches ultimate maturity when an atmosphere of trust and unselfishness exists among members. In such an environment, open communication and respect for opinions and rights of others are paramount. Since the only way to break down barriers to quality improvement is to gain greater insight and understanding of each person involved in the process, the team atmosphere is preferred. Teamwork is not only desired, it is required if meaningful change is to occur.

Since it's increasingly evident that the success of future quality improvement efforts in schools will depend to a large extent on the ability to create and foster cohesive teams of teachers, managers, and service staff, a further examination of the characteristics of productive teamwork is required.

To begin with, an atmosphere where people feel comfortable, confident, and motivated to do their job is crucial. In working toward team and overall school goals, the group needs to be recognized, have control and influence, and be involved in meaningful and relevant issues. These conditions will lead to effective team performance and be best accomplished when all members are treated equally by sharing responsibility and credit for all team accomplishments.

Teams must be built on trust, both among members of the team itself and in the school. Unless there is trust, it is fruitless to ask teachers and staff to contribute their ideas, energy, and time. Trust occurs more easily in a supportive environment where there is understanding and recognition that there will be differences of opinion. In such an atmosphere, risk taking is encouraged and failure is accepted.

Trust does not automatically occur when teams are organized; it develops over time. Included in the trust-building process is the need for a history of keeping commitments (small and large). Emphasis on the importance of trust comes from the realization by top management that teams can make things happen and cause meaningful and lasting change to occur. This trusting atmosphere begins by shifting from the traditional practice of "telling" to the preferred practice of "listening."

Lapses in management commitment or breakdowns in communication can cause trust to diminish. A top-level administrator who creates stress and worry in the organization through ineffective application of power can cause the whole system to weaken. It is essential, therefore, to constantly review management actions and continually evaluate the organization's climate.

Another condition for effective team involvement is the fostering of open communication across all levels of the organization. This requires good listening skills so that ideas of team members are heard and considered. It includes the sharing of information and an openness to suggestions, giving every person an opportunity to express opinions no matter how unrealistic those opinions may seem.

This communication process accepts disagreement among team members and encourages diverse ideas. In a highly participative, healthy team, conflict is handled in a constructive way and is not discouraged. The process fosters the clarification of issues, ideas, and suggestions. In the team setting, managers need to model their participatory behavior by accepting a role as an equal and not a dominating member of the team. Managers should nurture self-esteem among the team by ensuring that each member has the same opportunities to participate.

The team is built through careful planning and guidance. The highest priority should be given to fostering good team involvement through the manager's desire and commitment to increase quality improvement processes in the department. Without this, the process will break down.

Adequate training in team building and conflict resolution is necessary. Since managers use a variety of styles, people on both the lower and upper levels of the bureaucratic continuum receive filtered information about what is really going on. Reports to both groups sometimes carry omissions and/or distortions that include the things people want to hear. As a result, staff often get misinformation about top management expectations, and top management gets misinformation about activities in the program and service areas of the school. Through an intensive training program, managers learn to understand themselves better. They acquire team-building skills which break down these communication problems. They also learn how to deal with conflict and reach consensus when there is disagreement.

Teams are only as effective as the individual members and their willingness to get involved. David Grant, in his article "Being an Effective Member of a Work Group," lists factors necessary for good teamwork. Among them is the willingness of the team members to sacrifice for the benefit of others through a sharing of successes (and failures) and through compromise by abiding by decisions reached through consensus. In such an atmosphere, team members allow the team leader to head the group and determine the overall direction which the team takes. This includes contributing to the process and being willing to try something new.[7]

When FVTC decided to initiate work teams as a part of the quality process, team-building roles were identified. Included were the roles of the quality facilitator (team leader), the immediate supervisor, the measurement consultant, the team members themselves, and the college's quality coordinator. An outline of these roles can be found in Appendix C.

Types Of Teams

In FVTC's quality process model, several types of teams are advocated. They range from institutional-wide committees to small department work unit teams. The model also provides for ad hoc teams to be established as the need arises.

At the college, employees from all personnel levels are involved in various school-wide teams. The most visible of these teams are those associated with the quality process itself. The Total Quality Leadership Council is a district-wide team that serves as the key quality process planning and monitoring unit. It should serve as the model team for the organization. Several other institutional teams are included in the model. Rotation plans are used on these college-wide teams to encourage involvement of faculty and staff from different departments.

In addition to the district-wide teams, others are established in the various work units. No preferred pattern has emerged for the formation of these teams. Most teams are organized on a departmental basis with responsibilities for one or more related instructional programs or for one particular type of service. Various levels of personnel are members of these teams. The facilitator of the team is usually selected by the team members and the goals and decisions of the team are determined by consensus. Some teams are organized on a self-management basis. Information on this type of team is found in Chapter 6.

The activities of work unit teams are varied, but they are usually related to planning, establishing priorities, identifying issues, solving problems and taking corrective action, measuring and charting processes, and establishing and scheduling work assignments. More information on the process of problem identification and elimination is found in Chapter 8.

Some Reflections And Thoughts On Application

The organization and development of teams at FVTC can best be described as chaotic. In fact, an overall generalization might be that they were not very successful at all, at least at the start. This was especially true about the organization of some of the self-managed teams.

Our first attempt at establishing a self-managed team occurred about three years into the process. A pilot group in associate degree Nursing was chosen to become a self-managed team. Since there were some personnel problems in that department, we thought that the simplest solution was to allow the group to manage itself.

The dean of the division was not completely sold on the self-managed team idea, but she agreed to give it a try. Several meetings were held and the group became involved in the difficult challenge of defining work functions and determining responsibilities. Defining work functions was the easiest part; determining who would do what was not quite as simple. To begin with, the department coordinator was a reluctant participant; she saw this effort as a means to eliminate her position. Another major problem was that the group began the process of organizing the self-managed team without training in team building, communication, confrontation, and conflict resolution. As a result, the team stumbled along without much success, at least in the early months of the pilot.

About halfway through the process, the dean wisely sought assistance. She engaged the services of a consultant who conducted several training sessions. It was also decided to reassign the former manager of the department to other responsibilities. These measures helped but they could have been avoided with better planning. The department struggled and is now coping with the challenges that come with being the first.

A great deal was learned from this experience. First of all, we learned that self-managed teams should not be organized without intensive training in team building and other skills required to enhance team relationships. We also learned that work units should not be permitted to become self-directed without a careful analysis of the department culture. These questions should be answered before self-management work units are created:

- Is there management support for the idea of self-managed teams?

- Is the group ready for shared management responsibility?

- Has there been training in team building, confrontation exchanges, and conflict resolution?

- Can an atmosphere of trust, confidence, and loyalty be attained?

- Is the group willing to enter into this venture of risk, complex problem solving, and self-directed management?

The formation of other work unit teams in the college was less traumatic. Each division was asked to organize one or more work teams and identify and solve at least one problem. In all, 55 teams were established.

Our quality coordinator did an excellent job of defining roles of the various team participants. She arranged for special training in problem solving and the use of statistical process control techniques. Twenty-six people took the course, and they became the first "measurement consultants" for the college.

The coordinator also offered an introductory course in team building for all staff. Many staff participated in this preliminary training that focused on determining and understanding the various personality types of the team members.

The initial ventures into team formation and operation produced mixed results. There were several examples of successful problem identification and elimination. Measurement and charting activities took place throughout the organization as the teams became acquainted with statistical thinking approaches. Successful ventures usually focused on identifying and measuring barriers to providing quality-first service. Teams typically began by charting problems created by others outside the department. In a few cases, the team focused on the elimination of errors or problems which were created by the team members themselves.

Some of the initial team efforts were utter failures. Either they never got fully off the ground or the teams didn't continue to operate. Some met only once or twice—they looked at this as an organizational mandate and they didn't like the idea.

There are several reasons for these mixed results, and they can be categorized as follows:

- There was a lack of support and commitment by the immediate manager of the team.

- The team members didn't understand what they were to do.

- The team members looked upon this new initiative as a requirement which interfered with their regular work.

- There wasn't enough time for the teams to meet during their regularly assigned hours.

In spite of inconclusive results, most people close to the process feel that the use of teams is the only way to go. While we underestimated the need for commitment by immediate managers, their lack of support occurred primarily because they were not adequately prepared for what was to come. We learned that a formal orientation and training program in the use of teams is absolutely essential!

The time issue also needs to be addressed. It is unrealistic to expect faculty and staff to get enthused about team meetings when they are already busy with their regular work and with other new initiatives. The Total Quality Leadership Council endorsed the appointment of a two-member study team to examine this issue. This study was conducted by the faculty union president and a manager. Together, they planned, organized, and coordinated the study. Each was given half-time release from regular duties for six months to conduct the study and prepare a report with recommendations. Their recommendations related to the time issue are discussed in Chapter 7.

In spite of problems which came up, I'm encouraged by the successes which occurred. In several departments, excellent progress was made, and the teams continue to move forward to define and solve new problems. Their experiences convince me that the use of teams has great potential in schools.

Summary

Significant changes and innovation in education will not occur unless teachers and other staff are directly and actively involved in the planning and development of desired change. At FVTC, all school personnel are given opportunities to participate in the quality process through work unit teams.

The overall college team is responsible for global goals and strategic directions. Teams in the departments solve problems and improve processes. Smaller teams are best equipped to do this because they are normally closest to the unit of work and the actual processes.

There are certain conditions which maximize team involvement and effectiveness. The manager can help create that ideal environment and can foster cohesive teams of teachers, service staff, and managers. The perfect atmosphere is one where people feel comfortable, confident, and motivated to do their job. It is a supportive environment built on trust, understanding, and recognition that there will be differences of opinion. Risk taking and innovation are encouraged. At the center of it all is effective communication among all parties.

The team process focuses on the clarification of issues, ideas, and suggestions. Conflict is handled in a constructive way, and every person has opportunities to express opinions no matter how unrealistic they may seem. Because of the special skills needed by both the team members and their managers, adequate training in team building and conflict resolution is necessary.

Several types of teams are advocated, ranging from district-wide to small work unit teams. The quality improvement process usually requires several teams made up of personnel levels from the various departments of the school. Rotation plans are encouraged to give more people opportunities to be on a district quality committee.

CHAPTER 5

MAXIMIZING
CUSTOMER SATISFACTION

- Is education really a service?

- Do schools have customers like other businesses?

- Do school customers express dissatisfaction?

- Can the quality process significantly improve customer services?

These four questions should be answered with a resounding "yes." Education is a service with customers like any other business and those customers do, indeed, express satisfaction and dissatisfaction about school services and instruction. The quality process in education creates an awareness of customer needs and significantly improves the quality of services by meeting and exceeding expectations.

Since no business or school can be successful without customers, educators must understand what constitutes quality in the eyes of its past, current, and potential customers and then deliver what is necessary to meet and exceed those expectations. There is competition, even in public education, because students have different options regarding their education. In some states, there are legislative mandates in the K-12 system called "choice" programs. With "choice," parents and students select their preferred schools rather than be assigned. Students who want to acquire post-secondary education have numerous options available to them. Given different choices, students may decide on a school for the same reasons that customers choose a bank, doctor, insurance company, or hospital.

Just as in business and industry, the key to meeting customer satisfaction in education is to analyze why customer expectations have not been exceeded in the past. According to John Goodman, president of the Technical Assistance Research Program, most companies (and schools are included here) spend 95 percent of their customer service time fixing problems and only five percent identifying and analyzing them.[8] Since the key to any quality process is prevention of problems rather than correction later, educators must understand beforehand the nature of customer expectations.

According to Goodman, 50 percent of customers with problems will never complain to anyone, another 45 percent will complain to a front-line person (in education that's the teacher or service worker), and less than five percent will go directly to the school board or top school administrator. It can be concluded that for each problem which reaches the top, there are 19 others. "People don't complain," he says, "because it's too much hassle or because they feel nobody cares anyhow."[9]

Spencer Hutchins, Jr., president of the American Society for Quality Control (ASQC), reviewed the findings of the 1988 Gallup Poll on customer service and confirms some significant things which are also applicable to education:

- People will pay a high premium for what they perceive to be higher quality.

- About half of those who experience poor quality service do nothing about it.

- Customers identify the following as factors in high quality services: courtesy, promptness, a sense of needs being satisfied, and attitude of the service provider.

- Customers give the lowest quality rating to government agencies (which probably includes education).[10]

The quality process provides the mechanism to significantly improve customer service and exceed expectations of both internal and external customers. There are a number of steps in the FVTC quality process model which give this special attention:

- **Step 1, Management Commitment**—The school's CEO and other senior administrators should provide the leadership to instill a desire throughout the organization to determine and exceed customer requirements.

- **Step 4, Education and Training**—The formal education plan should include training for all employees in how to maximize services to both internal and external customers.

- **Step 8, Identify and Eliminate Problems**—An important part of the quality process is to identify and eliminate problems. The system should make it convenient and comfortable for people to identify those things which prevent them from doing their job right the first time. The improvement for the internal customers (all people in the organization), as well as the external customers, should be considered when identifying problems.

- **Step 9, Research and Develop New Initiatives**—The plan for research includes the collection and analysis of data on customer satisfaction. In education, this requires surveys among students, parents, employers, faculty and staff, and the community at large.

- **Step 12, Launch a Customer Revolution**—The use of techniques which leads to exceeding customer requirements should be included in the conforming requirements for this step in the model. The efforts of everyone in the school should be targeted at establishing, meeting, and exceeding customer requirements.

Since service is an organization's competitive advantage, recognize that people are its most important asset. The way staff are treated and the way they work together will determine how they treat their customers. Schools will significantly improve their service efforts if they focus greater attention on their front-line staff and if they establish processes and systems which:

- Ascertain customer needs, proactively measure their perceptions of service, and develop a customer information system.

- Decentralize responsibilities to ensure that front-line staff have the ability and authority to deviate from set practices and customize, as necessary, services for students.

- Design and implement a quality measurement system that tracks student service functions and provides feedback to both staff and students.

- Develop a hassle-free system to handle situations when customers perceive that they have received less service than they expected.

- Make one person responsible for overall customer service management and improvement to ensure that complaints are handled expeditiously without being transferred from department to department.

Defining School Customers

The first step when launching a customer service approach in education is to recognize that schools have customers just as business or industry does. While some educators have difficulty referring to students as customers, it's necessary that all who work in schools accept that type of reference. A total customer orientation puts a different focus on how students and coworkers are treated.

The primary external customers of schools are, of course, students who attend classes and use school services. Other external customers are those close to the students, including parents, spouses, and families, as well as employers who hire school graduates and taxpayers who contribute to financing the school.

Besides external customers, schools have internal customers who are their employees—instructors, teacher aides, support staff, technical staff, and managers. When a manager provides services to a teacher, the teacher becomes the manager's customer. A secretary who prepares a report is serving a customer—in this case, his or her boss. School administrators are customers when they receive services from a technical or service department of the school. As a result, the focus changes from serving a customer to being a customer depending on the circumstance.

The goal is to provide services which constantly exceed customer expectations. This requires the preparation of schoolwide conforming requirements which detail minimum expectations. The specifics for these requirements are defined in the Customer Service Quality Element. However, each service unit of the school prepares a list of separate standards which they seek to meet when providing services within their department.

Determining Customer Requirements And Expectations

There are numerous ways to determine customer expectations. The most obvious way is to sit down with customers and talk about what is expected. Satisfaction surveys should be conducted, but asking customers if they are satisfied in a survey generally isn't enough because surveys don't generally identify customer expectations and they don't assess performance relative to competitors.

A useful technique to determine customer expectations is analysis of competitors using a process called "competitive benchmarking." This system is designed to assess the competition and use that knowledge to implement plans to assume leadership in the market. Xerox defines competitive benchmarking as "the continuous process of measuring products, services, and practices against the toughest competitors or companies renowned as the leaders."[11]

The goal of competitive benchmarking is to attain superiority in quality services, costs, and customer satisfaction. It is an effort to get and keep the competitive advantage through the collection of data about competitors and application of the analysis of that data to your own operation. It is a means of exceeding customer expectations by assuming leadership from the most challenging of competitors. Once information about competitors is collected and analyzed, the organization establishes its own benchmarks as goals to achieve—thereby exceeding competitor advantages. Competitive benchmarking is a cyclical process which requires continual review and analysis and constant modification of goals (your own benchmarks).

Schools can also use benchmarking. In the K-12 system, test scores may be the benchmark calibrated to determine where the school ranks in relation to other schools. Other benchmark information may include course fees, costs per student, faculty/staff compensation, and student entrance and exit grade point averages. At FVTC, teams of faculty and staff visit schools identified as benchmark colleges to examine programs and services such as prevocational assessment, technology transfer, and computer integrated manufacturing. The focus is then to match and exceed competitor benchmark standards.

Other Determinants Of Quality

In the magazine *Journal of Marketing*, Parasuraman, Zeithami, and Berry cite several determinants of quality which customers use when evaluating services. These include company reliability, responsiveness, competence, access, courtesy, and communications. In addition, the authors identify trustworthiness, honesty, and security for customers (things such as safety and financial independence). They feel that knowing and understanding customers is a part of learning what their requirements are and providing individual attention to exceeding expectations. Other tangible determinants such as aesthetics, appearance of personnel, type of equipment, and other physical evidences of service were identified.[12]

In a survey conducted by ASQC and the Gallup Organization, Inc., consumers' perceptions concerning the quality of American products and services were measured based on interviews with 1,005 adults, 18 years or older. Table 5.1 shows the characteristics of a high quality service rated by those interviewed.

Those who responded ranked items such as courteous/polite treatment, promptness, and attitude of personnel highest. Conversely, items such as company name, no mistakes, and convenience were ranked at the bottom.[13]

Question: How do you determine the quality of services rather than products?

Determine quality by...	All Consumers 1985 %	All Consumers 1988 %
Courteous/polite treatment	21	21
Satisfy your needs	18	13
Past experience/trial and error	13	6
Recommendations/word of mouth	12	8
Promptness	12	15
Price	11	7
Attitude of personnel	10	12
Helpful personnel	9	8
Friendliness	8	8
Reputation	7	5
Personal attention	6	5
Cleanliness	6	7
Availability	4	3
Services are good	4	6
Efficiency	4	8
Trouble free	4	1
Convenience	3	2
Dependability	3	6
Company name	2	1
Variety of services offered	2	2
Accuracy	2	2
Miscellaneous	4	2
Don't know	8	13

* Banks, hotels, and hospitals receive the highest satisfaction ratings among seven types of service rated by respondents. Auto repair and local government service receive the lowest ratings.

Table 5.1 – Characteristics of High Quality Service
('88 Gallup Survey – 1,005 Respondents)

Listed below are some examples of customer requirements identified by the Customer Service Committee at FVTC.

Customer requirements from taxpayers

- The costs per student will be maintained at the average level of statewide school districts of the same size.

- Student/teacher ratios will be maintained at the average level of statewide school districts of the same size.

- Faculty and staff compensation will be equal to schools of similar size and mission.

Customer requirements from employers

- Graduates will be technically competent to perform job tasks as identified by competency lists which are criterion referenced and determined by using business and industry input.

- Graduates will demonstrate positive job attitudes as well as continuous quality improvement competencies.

Customer requirements from school employees

- All school employees will have opportunities to submit Continuous Process Improvement (CPI) forms and receive a response within three working days.

- All school employees will have opportunities to complete an annual organizational climate survey and receive the results on a work unit and school-wide basis within three months after the survey is conducted.

- All school employees will be appropriately recognized for their contribution to the success of the school.

Continuous Process Improvement

When there are obstacles to improving customer service and getting the job done right the first time, an internal climate must be established to encourage the identification of those obstacles and initiation of action to cause their permanent removal. The Continuous Process Improvement (CPI) system at FVTC encourages this to happen. This process provides opportunities for internal personnel to improve their performance to their customers while increasing their job satisfaction.

The CPI process is a simple reporting system with a monitoring feature. Employees identify obstacles to getting the job done right the first time by completing a three-part form and submitting copies to the immediate supervisor and the school CPI Coordinator. The supervisor has three working days to issue a written response back to the filer which provides either an immediate solution or an indication that some type of action will be forthcoming. Most problems can be solved right in the work unit. Using problem-solving and measurement/charting techniques which are explained in Chapter 8, staff has a systematic way to improve processes and make sure that the activity being measured remains under control.

A CPI coordinator is appointed to perform the functions related to the position. One of the most important tasks is to track and monitor CPI forms. The tracking system used at FVTC is computer-based with a mechanized filing feature. Through this system, CPIs can be filed and ticklers, or reminder notices, attached and reported in a number of categories. In this way, CPIs are monitored by work unit code, classification category, and level of solution. The CPI coordinator maintains this system and also makes personal contacts with the filer of the CPI and the respective supervisor.

The CPI coordinator provides ongoing orientation and training for school managers to ensure that the process is understood. The goal is to have managers and others use the CPI process as a prevention tool. It is necessary, therefore, for managers to provide a sound system which promotes confidentiality. When the CPI coordinator gives reports to the Total Quality Leadership Council, care should be taken to avoid identifying the work unit or supervisors who are impacted by CPIs which have been filed.

During the first three years of the CPI process a FVTC, a total of 178 CPI forms were filed. These were reported in five different classifications as identified in Figure 5.1. Of the 178 CPIs originally filed, one remains unresolved, one was dropped by the filer, four were referred to corrective action, and several are still being modified.

December 1, 1987 to June 30, 1990

Classification Type	Number
Communications	19
Human Resources	11
Material Resources	32
Policies and Procedures	69
Work Environment	47
TOTAL CPIs	**178**

Figure 5.1 – Continuous Process Improvements Forms Filed

Corrective Action Process

The Corrective Action (CA) process analyzes problems which hinder quality and initiates action to correct these problems. The CA process is used when problems identified through CPIs cannot be worked out at the work unit level because changes are required across the organization.

A Corrective Action Committee is formed with representation from each personnel level of the school. It meets as often as necessary depending on the number and type of CPIs referred for action. Usually the CA committee will appoint an ad hoc CA team (CAT) to study a specific problem and come up with a recommended solution. The CAT is comprised of members from throughout the organization who are involved in the problem. Once the problem is resolved, the CAT is disbanded.

Suggestion Boxes

Another way to identify problems is through the use of suggestion boxes. Students and staff are given opportunities to compliment individuals or departments who have provided excellent service, or they may use this means to identify problems and voice complaints. This can be effective if the system is carefully monitored and if there is assurance that quick action will be taken to respond to both suggestions and complaints.

A suggestion box system was put into effect at FVTC in early 1990. As of December 1990, 179 forms were deposited into 15 suggestion boxes located throughout the campuses. Sixty-five percent of the forms were submitted by students and twenty percent were completed by staff. The rest were filed by visitors to the college.

Comment forms are collected each day and sent to the appropriate department for information or action. If the person identifies himself or herself on the form, a member of the Customer Service Committee contacts them personally.

The majority of the concerns or suggestions received focused on these four categories: (1) facilities; (2) curriculum issues; (3) staffing; (4) food service.

Not all concerns or suggestions were major and not all were corrected. Some of the action taken as a result of this process is as follows:

- A noisy door in the library was fixed

- Weekly food menus are now published

- A list of electives for accounting majors was developed and distributed to students

- Heating and ventilation problems were addressed in C building at the main campus

- Additional lounge furniture was purchased

- A potential hazard at the front entrance was corrected

- A daily newsletter was established

Focus Groups

Another effective technique of soliciting customer expectations involves the use of focus groups. A school representative meets with a representative group of customers and asks for their assistance to improve processes. The suggestions are then summarized and presented to the proper department for action.

At FVTC we have used focus groups in a variety of situations, including the following:

- **Student Services Focus Group**—This focus group reviewed the variety of services ranging from admissions to placement to assist the student services staff in improving their services.

- **Adult Student Focus Group**—Students over age 40 discussed the barriers they faced in pursuing technical college education and how FVTC could be more effective in helping adult students overcome barriers.

- **Employer Focus Group on the Aging Work Force**—District employers discussed how they are coping with aging work forces and how the technical college could help them with training and retraining aging employees.

- **Staff Focus Groups on Enrollment Management Plan**—Three staff focus groups reacted to an enrollment management plan developed from task force reports they had written earlier.

- **Focus Groups on Guaranteed Retraining Policy**—Two staff groups and one student group gave their opinion and suggestions for a school policy to guarantee retraining for graduates who do not get jobs in their field of study.

- **Employee Focus Group on Self-Managed Teams**—Those employees involved in teams voiced their concerns and suggestions for improving the use of self-managed teams at the college.

- **Focus Group on Publications**—Students gave their reaction to a publication that included a daily calendar, information guide to student activities, and key school dates.

In addition to these focus groups, one of the instructional divisions has established a Student Advisory Committee. James Pierce, dean of the Business and Marketing Division, meets once a month with several students who represent each of the programs in his division. Issues are identified before the meeting and an agenda is published. As the issues are handled, a report that indicates what has happened is circulated to the entire staff.

Handling Complaints

No matter how hard school personnel try to maximize customer services and meet expectations, there will always be students and other customers who are dissatisfied. Providing good customer service includes the successful handling of complaints. Complaints should be viewed in a positive way, for each one is an opportunity to correct a problem and eliminate it forever.

Less than 10 percent of dissatisfied customers file formal complaints. If that's true, 90 percent of the unsatisfied customers never bother to complain. Instead, these unhappy customers go elsewhere and tell several other people about the service problem, so the effect is multiplied.

In order to fully maximize services to students, the Customer Service Committee at FVTC feel that it is critical to handle complaints positively. They believe that it is better to hear complaints than lose students, and they have developed guidelines to successfully deal with these unhappy people. Noel/Levitz, a consulting firm from Iowa, offers several ideas for effectively handling complaints.

They recommend handling problems by focusing on solving the complaint rapidly rather than taking it personally. They suggest a courteous and helpful attitude and recommend that the angry customer be given an apology or an explanation as quickly as possible. They recommend thanking the person who complains for bringing the problem to light.

Noel/Levitz recommends patience and tact even when the person complaining is making outrageous statements. They suggest techniques which try to get the customer to work with, rather than against, the employee. They recommend being warm, sincere, and empathetic, and urge solving the problem as soon as possible. Effective communications and good listening skills (putting yourself in the customer's place) are suggested to diffuse the situation. They emphasize trying to "solve the problem" and view the complaint as being positive rather than negative.[14]

Some Reflections And Thoughts On Application

Customer service improvement can be implemented very early in the quality improvement process. Once staff members accept the idea that they are serving customers just as businesses do, it is easy to put processes in place toward the goal of maximizing customer satisfaction. A first step is to have each department write conforming requirements for serving their customers. Providing training in customer service for all front-line people in the school is also important.

For some reason, FVTC did not put major focus on customer service improvement in the beginning. Maybe it was because we assumed we were providing excellent service already. Or, it could have been that our original model did not have a process step which dealt directly with customer service. In any event, when we designed our own quality improvement model, we added a process step and established a Customer Service Committee. That committee was the first at FVTC to include student members. The committee wrote the Customer Service Quality Element (see Appendix J) and outlined the district conforming requirements which became the measurement criteria for meeting or exceeding the requirements.

Once the committee was established, we quickly moved forward to make up for lost time. Robert Darula, dean of student services, set up several focus groups to get suggestions from students on how to improve services. Several changes were made. In addition, our dean of business education established a Student Advisory Committee which meets monthly to offer recommendations.

As a part of our Phase II training program for service staff, we are including special instruction in customer service. The training also includes ways to improve handling customer complaints. The Noel/Levitz Customer Service Training Program book *Connections* is used to complement the training. We have also appointed a customer service manager who is responsible for assisting staff in placing major emphasis on delighting customers of the college.

We plan to continue using the results of the annual "Student Satisfaction Survey" to monitor our progress in exceeding customer expectations through exemplary service.

The Noel/Levitz customer service training manual for student employees, *Partners*, is used to train all work study students, interns, and auxiliary student workers.

A customer service focus has immediate and visible results and is relatively easy to initiate. Its impact on customer service is apparent right away.

Summary

It is not enough to just satisfy customers. The goal must be to maximize customer satisfaction by constantly delighting customers and exceeding their expectations. One way to do this is to carefully identify all customers being served, find out what constitutes quality in their eyes, and then deliver what is necessary to exceed their expectations.

The quality process model designed at FVTC provides the framework for maximizing customer satisfaction in schools. Of the 16 steps in the model, five have requirements for directly addressing customer service. Step 12 (Launch a Customer Revolution) focuses on customer service.

We have identified external customers (students, parents or spouses, employers, taxpayers) and internal customers (all employees and board members). Conforming requirements have been written for each category of customers and they become the goals of customer service— with the ultimate target of constantly exceeding requirements.

This chapter suggests that one way to establish customer service goals is to collect data about competitors and analyze it to establish higher customer service targets. Reviewing determinants of quality which customers identify when evaluating school services is also helpful.

Since it is essential that internal customers (employees) receive quality service that exceeds their expectations, it is necessary to define their requirements. This should be done in each service department. There should also be a formal process to give school workers the opportunity to identify obstacles to completing their work right the first time. The system proposed is the Continuous Process Improvement (CPI) and Corrective Action (CA) process. These processes provide opportunities for employees to receive assistance which will improve the quality of their services.

Finally, this chapter suggests handling complaints in a proactive way by viewing complaints as a positive means of improving services to customers.

CHAPTER 6

QUALITY-BASED SCHOOL MANAGEMENT

Quality improvement in education should not be viewed as a "quick fix" process. It is a long-term effort which requires organizational change and restructuring. Raising the level of management awareness is prerequisite to initiating and sustaining the effort. It begins with teaching managers basic quality concepts. They must understand the definition of quality and appreciate its full implications to the long-term success of the school. Most importantly, managers must identify with and be comfortable with their role in the quality improvement process.

Commitment to the quality improvement process by managers is essential and must be obvious to the entire staff. Visible actions of school managers send an unmistakable message to the organization about what is important and where the manager's priorities lie. In too many schools, management responsibility is implicit rather than explicit. Quality improvement is simply too important to imply responsibility for it to occur.

The quality improvement process provides the vehicle to create the type of cultural change which is necessary for change in education. This requires a review of the way schools have been managed and movement toward greater involvement by all who are associated with the school. The management function moves from one that was closed, autocratic, and hierarchical to one that is open, participatory, enabling, and horizontal.

Cultural changes are advocated in this model with special attention given to the role and function of school managers. It suggests an integration system which, over time, will impact on each and every management process there is.

Because formal quality techniques are not practiced by most school managers, they may be uncomfortable when they hear about the idea. The implementation of quality improvement processes usually does not mean radically changing ways of doing things. It calls for good leadership in each work unit of the school with common goals, recognition, and participation by everyone in the unit. It requires teamwork, cooperation, and above all, good communication. It means involving people in decisions, encouraging participation in problem solving, sharing information, and providing constructive feedback to everyone.

Therefore, the quality process recognizes and capitalizes on the contributions of all in the school: teachers, support staff, technical staff, counselors, and managers. It does so while raising everyone's level of commitment with the manager right in the middle of it all. The manager's role during this transformation shifts from that of an enforcer or director to that of a facilitator who educates, advises, empowers, enables, and supports staff. In effect, it calls for establishing a new management culture for the school.

In this new environment, management patterns must be evident and visible. Problem solving and measurement becomes routine and the manager's responsibilities become clearer and less ambiguous. Immediate attention by managers is required to meet and exceed customers' requirements.

Cultural Transformation Of Schools

While most educational reforms have mandated changes in schools, their focus generally has been to maintain typical hierarchical school structures. Some reformers, however, have called for massive restructuring of schools. Mary Hatwood Futrell, former president of the National Education Association, says that the new changes require "democratic reforms that enhance the decision-making authority of classroom teachers and building administrators." She calls for "cultures of cooperation by all who have a stake—teachers, administrators, students, parents, school board members, and business and community leaders."[15]

When schools decide to shift to these new styles that include more people in more decisions, the results can add up to a cultural shock for the institution. Tom Peters warns of this turmoil in his book *Thriving on Chaos*.[16] Several other authors support the contention that the process of changing management philosophy in any organization creates special challenges for those in charge. They contend that people in middle-management roles, such as principals, vice principals, technical managers, and coordinators, may find the process outright traumatic!

Typical School Organization

When schools were first organized in this country, they had little organizational structure. Typically, the school board hired a superintendent or school headmaster/headmistress, and he or she hired other teachers needed to instruct and manage the school. In the one-room school, the teacher was totally responsible for all activities related to the education and that included everything from starting the fire on cold days to teaching and counseling students and reporting to the school board.

As communities grew and schools consolidated, more administrators were added. Soon there were principals, associate principals, librarians, counselors, department chairs, and other types of managers who assisted the superintendent. Superintendents of large districts began to surround themselves with top-level administrators with expertise in areas such as business and financial management, personnel services, and academic affairs. Other service and technical managers were added as technology crept into education and media and computers became teaching tools for teachers.

Following the launching of Sputnik by the Russians in 1957, the United States Congress passed the National Defense Education Act, which provided for greater emphasis in mathematics, science, and technical education. In addition, the legislation provided funds for massive counselor training across the country. As counselors entered our schools, the roles of the principals and other school managers changed. Counselors assumed, in addition to their guidance and counseling duties, management-type functions such as student scheduling, teacher assignments, and room utilization. Their management responsibilities often consumed more time than their counseling and guidance functions.

By the 1960s, schools had become so specialized in their approaches to performing services that there often were as many administrators, managers, counselors, coordinators, principals, technical staff, and other support personnel as there were teachers. There were so many different types and combinations of managers and specialists that it was often difficult to determine ratios between management and faculty. This caused board members and faculty unions to question the numbers and types of noninstructional personnel. It became even more confusing when some managers were accreted into bargaining units with teachers. These endless levels of faculty, staff, and administrators organized in hierarchical structures were often five or more levels of management away from students. In such an environment, school administrators often acted like master journeymen, telling their apprentices what to do. To complicate matters, school administrators were often lacking in management skills because they were usually former teachers who had little management experience.

The situation has led to numerous calls for reform during the last decade. A number of "save our school" movements occurred and legislators, business leaders, parents, and union leaders began calling for action. In a rare display of unanimity, executives, educators, and politicians began to call for a complete restructuring of the American school system. Former Secretary of Education William Bennett called for reforms "approaching a revolution." Union leaders Albert Shanker of the American Federation of Teachers (AFT) and Mary Hatwood Futrell of the National Education Association (NEA) both agreed that fundamental changes were needed. However, they cautioned that teachers must be a part of any planning for any new system in education.[17]

The Quality Process And School Management

The quality improvement process provides a viable framework for designing the cultural changes and processes needed for meaningful change in education. The framework advocates the use of private sector methods to transform the management of schools. It provides the impetus to systematic and continual change which focuses on the needs of both external customers (students, taxpayers, parents, and politicians) and internal customers (teachers, managers, and support staff).

All successful quality improvement programs in the private sector require management involvement, problem solving, statistical thinking, measurement, and recognition of employees. The same components are needed in education. This requires fundamental changes in the management of schools which are similar to the reforms made in Japan during the past 40 years and those now entering business and industry in the United States. These same principles of quality and productivity that have been successful in the private sector can be applied to schools in these ways.

1. Increased involvement by faculty and staff in the management and decision making of the schools.

2. More authority and responsibility delegated to levels of expertise in the schools.

3. Greater autonomy for individual schools and more latitude for individual departments.

4. Increased faculty and staff professional development and training.

5. School decisions based on customer requirements and data collection, using scientific methods and statistical analysis.

6. Improved leadership skills for those in management positions.

7. Innovative participatory techniques rather than condescending autocratic methods of management.

8. Continued commitment to quality, with concern for excellence in all processes of the school.

9. School practices and decisions based on customer needs as depicted in quality elements with accompanying conforming requirements.

10. Continued analysis of how well the new methods are working.[18]

The process of involving individuals in implementing change and in making decisions at the lowest possible levels has also been called school-based management. When decisions are made at lower levels, they flow up through the system rather than down from the superintendent's or principal's office. Teachers solve problems related to instruction and curriculum, and custodians make decisions about maintenance problems.

In a pamphlet titled "School-Based Management: A Strategy for Better Learning," the major leadership organizations of American PK-12 schools state that this new type of management requires that "those most closely affected by decisions ought to play an important part in making those decisions." The article argues that such reforms will be accepted when "carried out by the people who feel a sense of ownership and responsibility for the process."[19]

Traditional School Management

While there has been creative and progressive leadership in many schools, some districts still operate using traditional management approaches. In such schools, the work generally gets accomplished without major conflict. School administrators often act as arbitrators, judges, or umpires. They usually work long hours and attempt to do the bulk of the managerial paperwork. They are constantly putting out brush fires and holding meetings with staff which can best be described as "classical drags." At those meetings, extraneous concerns by faculty and staff typically dominate the discussions and seldom are the major school issues debated and brainstormed.

As in traditional business and industry organizations, everything in schools is generally pushed up the hierarchical ladder for decisions, with numerous bottlenecks along the way. Sometimes managers feel that they must know about everything going on in their department to be in constant control of things. If the manager is responsible for everything, he or she usually attempts to solve all problems. This results in managerial dominance over everything that happens. With this total authority and responsibility, some people (including managers themselves) may feel the manager is infallible and the most creative person in the department. The system itself implies that the managers have greater technical expertise than those they supervise. In such a setting, the manager often feels he or she must take over all projects and come up with the resources and right answers needed to make things operate.[20] This traditional system promotes hero-type projects with the manager supposedly in complete charge of things.

Meanwhile, faculty and technical staff feel responsible only for the classes they teach and the curriculum they use or the services they provide. Since the manager is perceived as the solver of most problems, teachers and support staff are usually not emotionally committed to the goals of the department or the organization. Most projects are handled by the managers with limited involvement and communication with teachers and support staff. Because of this, teachers rarely have opportunities to meet with managers who are busy with their projects. This results in speculation by management that there is a lack of motivation by the faculty. The staff may even be thought of as being incompetent, lazy, and not interested. At the same time, faculty perceive managers as frustrated people, who are in the center of action but unable to get things done effectively. An air of passivity exists among the faculty and support staff and there is little motivation because meaningful changes generally cannot occur without prior approval by managers. Since little trust exists among the various levels in school, information is often not shared, and there is little teamwork.

Leadership Through Empowerment And Enhancement

In the quality-based approach, school leadership relies on the empowerment of teachers and others involved in the teaching/learning process. Teachers share in decision making and assume greater responsibilities. They are given more power to act and greater autonomy in most everything they do. Ernest Boyer, a former United States Commissioner of Education and current president of the Carnegie Foundation for the Advancement of Teaching, is an outspoken advocate of greater teacher authority. He reminds educators that most reforms have been imposed from the top down and most have failed. He contends that meaningful change will not occur until those involved, mostly teachers, feel the need to change. "Whatever is wrong with America's schools cannot be fixed without the help of those inside the classroom," Boyer said; and he added, "Yet in most states, teachers have been front-row spectators in a reform movement in which signals are being called by governors, legislators, state educational officials, and others far removed from the field of action."[21]

Many principles of leadership currently used in business and industry could be transplanted to education. They are identified by Casanova in her article, "Research and Practice: We Can Integrate Them," as follows:

1. School problems must be addressed by more people at each level in the school through an examination of all processes.

2. Team members should share in management responsibilities and school leaders should build effective work relationships through lateral and upward management.

3. Leaders must become supportive and inspirational and influence decisions without expressing total control.

4. Leaders should acquire new personal disciplines for problem solving and use statistical thinking techniques in decision making.

5. The leader's goal should be to assist people to reach their maximum potential. This results in more respect for individuals, a commitment to excellence, and a rejection of anything less.

6. School leaders should think longer term, look beyond the unit they are heading, and think in terms of constant renewal for both the individual and the organization.[22]

School administrators and middle managers, therefore, hold the key to the success of creating a new school environment through quality. In their pivotal role, they can do a number of things which will empower teachers, technical workers, and others. Managers can do this by:

1. Involving teachers and all staff in problem-solving activities, using basic scientific methods and the principles of statistical quality and process control.

2. Asking them how they think about things and how projects can be handled rather than telling them how they will happen.

3. Sharing as much management information as possible to help foster their commitment.

4. Asking staff which systems and procedures are preventing them from delivering quality to their customers—students, parents, coworkers.

5. Understanding that the desire for meaningful improvement of teachers is not compatible with a top-down approach to management.

6. Rejuvenating professional growth by moving responsibility and control for professional development directly to teachers and technical workers.

7. Implementing systematic and continued communication among everyone involved in schools.

8. Developing skills in conflict resolution, problem solving, and negotiations while displaying greater tolerance for and appreciation of conflict.

9. Being helpful without having all the answers and without being condescending.

10. Providing education in quality concepts and subjects such as team building, process management, customer service, communications, and leadership.

11. Modeling, by personally exhibiting desired characteristics and spending time walking around, listening to teachers and other customers.

12. Learning to be more like a coach and less like a boss.

13. Providing autonomy and allowing risk taking while being fair and compassionate.

14. Engaging in the delicate balancing act of ensuring quality to external customers (students, parents, taxpayers), while at the same time paying attention to the needs of internal customers (teachers, board members, and other coworkers).

In all of this, leadership requires a particular set of skills, knowledge, and attitudes directed toward helping others develop the same characteristics. The leader guides and empowers others while allowing them to advance themselves in their positions. In this shared-responsibility style, school managers defuse their own roles and create an interactive work environment. This style emphasizes neither leaders nor followers and puts multiple people in charge, rather than only a few.

The Upside-Down Paradigm

Karl Albrecht, in his book *At America's Service*, proposes a service-management concept using a model with a new, broader paradigm. While the model is not specifically designed for schools, the concepts apply. The model provides the framework for thinking about the overall organization and causing it to work on behalf of the mission and purpose of the organization. The concept proposed by Albrecht is contained in the model which has been adapted to education; Figure 6.1 shows this modification.

TRADITIONAL CONCEPTS	◄──── FOCUS ────►	FVTC MANAGEMENT CONCEPTS
Number of FTE Students, Faculty, and Staff (Student/Teacher Management Ratios)	**Educational Economics**	Meeting Needs of Internal and External Customers
Activities which Focus on Job Descriptions, Standards of Performance, and Objectives	**Management Work Focus**	Outcomes which Focus on Quality of Customers' Experiences
Measurement of Outcomes Related to Educational Economics	**Measurement Criteria**	Quality Elements: - Evidence of Customer Satisfaction - Organization Climate - Student Satisfaction - Employee Satisfaction
Control through Issuance of Procedures, Policies, and Directives	**Management Focus**	Enablement, Support, Empowerment, and Caring Assistance
Management Driven Hierarchical Structure	**Organization Focus**	Service Driven Horizontal Structure with Support and Resources to Those Closest to Customer
Management Through Chain of Command	**CEO Focus**	Creating and Maintaining a Quality First Culture

Figure 6.1 – Albrecht's Management Model Adapted to Education

The adapted model illustrates the difference between quality service management in education and traditional school management. This paradigm shift is revolutionary in that the emphasis is changed from the usual educational outcome orientation to a customer service model. According to Albrecht, this change turns the traditional pyramid of authority upside down with customers at the top and managers at the bottom. Albrecht's pyramid is shown in Figure 6.2, with educational personnel inserted.[23]

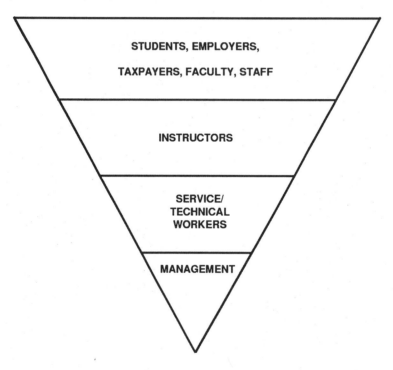

Figure 6.2 – Albrecht's Upside-Down Pyramid Adapted to Education

Transforming Management – The Results

When staff are involved in the shaping and monitoring of new plans, they are more willing to buy into continued involvement and commitment. This creates marked changes in the morale and attitudes of teachers and others—resulting in improved conditions for students. Principals and supervisors have more time for facilitating creativity and innovation. New activities, such as brainstorming meetings and creativity sessions, focus on eliminating customer barriers.

In such a mutually supportive environment, teachers and managers realize that their individual successes are interlocked with team action—their achievements rise and fall together. By loosening the management reins, teachers get new opportunities to manage themselves, doing what is necessary to get the job done. While this implementation requires profound school readjustment, the concept is simple. With the assistance of their managers, staff define, direct, evaluate, and communicate their own activities. Progressive, new leadership concepts such as integrating, envisioning, and synergizing replace controlling, directing, deciding, and executing.

Quality-based managers think less in hierarchical terms and more in horizontal ways which emphasize lateral integration. They become much more than just the next person in the chain of command. They learn that to earn the loyalty of and have credibility with those on their team, they must negotiate a fair, open, and mutually beneficial exchange between themselves and their team members. The use of teams frees managers to interface with others in the organization and foster innovation and change.

This new type of school management does not require a complete abdication of authority by those hired to provide school leadership. While the role of school managers changes, the need for leadership does not. There may be fewer levels of managers and more technical workers and specialists, but the principals, supervisors, and managers become even more important because of their need to coordinate the efforts of teams. The manager has to be both less active and more active at the same time.

Recruiting and hiring of top-notch staff is one of the most critical activities of the school leader. Futuristic managers do not wait around for someone to retire or leave and then hurry to fill the vacancy. They are constantly on the lookout for people with talents to enhance their team. They make contacts and seek out the right people to have people in line for positions in the department they manage. They have a skills inventory on hand at all times and often bring new staff aboard on a part-time basis—just to keep them in line for full-time positions. When someone leaves, the job is analyzed to determine if the position should be changed. Great emphasis is placed on proper screening, selection, and orientation of new employees.

Once a new staff member is hired, the manager has the responsibility to ensure that that person becomes an integrated member of the team. The manager instructs the new person on the mission and purpose of the school and orients the new person about the quality first process. In this way, the manager ensures that the new worker learns and uses the customer service techniques.

Since the manager wants his or her team to perform as a cohesive, autonomous unit, the focus on teamwork is paramount. The manager learns that to delegate effectively, he or she must engage in a carefully thought-out process that involves improving both the team and the individual.

However, this new culture does not call for the elimination of organizational structures with teachers and staff going off and doing whatever they want. Rather, the staff of Goodmeasure, Inc., a management consulting firm in Massachusetts, suggests that these new cultures require a clear structure to enable people to work within established boundaries in autonomous and creative ways.

In their work with a number of firms, the Goodmeasure staff have found that to improve quality and leadership it is necessary to establish ground rules up-front or the team will waste time. Because total freedom does not usually work effectively, the school manager stays involved with the team and remains available to support the team members, view results, and redirect or reorient as necessary. The manager also serves as the contact point with other school departments. In that role, he or she assists in coordinating team activities throughout the school. According to the Goodmeasure staff, managers have specific responsibilities to help their team solve problems. They contend that the manager:

- Is responsible for supervising the team, especially when the team crosses boundaries or work areas.

- Allocates necessary resources and supports the team as needed.

- Keeps the team informed about changes and new issues.

- Reviews the team's recommendations and decides what to do with them—implement, send back for modification, or send upward for approval, if necessary.

- Recognizes the work of the team and individual members and rewards them accordingly.[24]

Self-Management Teams

While there are a variety of structures in which teams are used, one interesting approach is the use of autonomous, self-managed teams. These groups require a shift in focus from individual to group methods of performing work. Such groups are characterized by a high degree of team decision making with emphasis on control from within, rather than from outside the team.

Self-management is the most highly participative of all team approaches. Its worthwhile goals are improved productivity, better quality, and reduced conflict in the department. There are few such groups in the United States and most are in manufacturing environments. At FVTC, the nursing and accounting departments have been reorganized using the self-management approach. In such a work unit, the role of the manager changes dramatically.

A study reported in the "Administrative Quarterly" found ambiguity in what the managers were actually contributing to the self-management team. The dominant role of the external manager is to lead others to lead themselves. With the shift in control from the leader to the followers, behaviors identified as being significant to the leader were:

- Encouragement of group self-reinforcement.

- Encouragement of self-criticism.

- Encouragement of goal setting.

- Encouragement of self-observation and self-evaluation.

- Encouragement of high expectations of performance.

- Encouragement of rehearsal before performing a task.[25]

While the role of the manager in this self-management system appears to be minimal, it is critical to the overall success of the team. The manager provides the vision from outside the team, while focusing on internal operations of the group. By encouraging constructive self-management worker behaviors, the manager positively relates to the overall effectiveness of the entire organization.

The use of self-managed teams in education offers the potential to impact positively on school improvement. Autonomous teams of teachers assuming major responsibility in instructional management matters will be successful when the manager is likewise effective in both defining and carrying out his or her role in such a system. There are usually elected team leaders within the self-management group and the manager needs special skills to identify the roles of each member, especially at the start of the new system. While the manager is less directive, he or she will nonetheless be visible and remain in charge. Techniques such as questioning, encouraging, and coaching team members will be useful in this new management style. The goal is to influence the team to do things themselves while fostering independence among the members. The ultimate function of the manager becomes teaching others to lead themselves.

Changing Management Styles

It's a major challenge to change management styles toward the model suggested. Most school managers and administrators have spent many years using autocratic approaches they have learned over the years. As a result, a manager with several years of experience in traditional approaches to school management will have as many years of old habits to dispose of. The leadership concepts implied in this model require a lengthy period of reorientation and training. While this all takes time, some things can be done immediately.

To begin, the commitment of the top administrator is essential to set the stage for the changes being advocated. The CEO must make it clear that new roles are required. Since many school managers have used various forms of participatory management effectively in the past, the adjustment may be relatively easy. For some, however, it may be difficult and take longer. The CEO plays a major role in assisting those who have difficulty with the new styles of management.

An important way in which the CEO can cause changes in management styles in the school is to become a role model. By setting examples, he or she encourages others to try these new approaches. Once managers know that they will be held accountable for promoting this type of change, the adaptation will begin. The use of special recognition programs may also be useful to encourage managers to change.

However, even with the full implementation of quality first processes in a school, change comes slowly. Great patience and understanding is required by both the leader and his or her customers. This cultural transformation will grow and reinforce itself as the reform begins to show positive results. The change will have such an impact on the organization that it will become a force that grows constantly and moves the school forward.

Some Reflections And Thoughts On Application

The need to orient and train existing administrators and managers in the new management approaches was underestimated at FVTC. I thought that managers would pick this up by themselves through reading about the new concepts. I didn't realize that our managers probably believed that the quality initiative was something that would soon go away and we would revert to our old ways. I also didn't realize that these new concepts created fear among some managers.

I don't think our managers appreciated it either when they kept hearing from me and others that 80 percent of the quality problems were the result of poor management practices. They became irritated when staff they supervised reminded them of that statistic. It didn't help matters when top-level administrators began to communicate directly to more front-line staff, including faculty. Managers felt left out of the process and, in retrospect, I can't blame them.

Even though managers were the first group to be trained, they only received 20 hours of formal training and most of it was simply an orientation to quality concepts. They received no initial training in problem-solving, team development, and statistical thinking approaches. Very little was done to prepare them for the trauma which was to come. When they heard that our general plan was to have fewer school managers in the future, they probably became fearful about their jobs. It didn't matter when I assured them that they had security and positions would not be eliminated except through attrition.

It was especially difficult for the middle managers who were directly above teachers on the organizational charts. To begin with, they were working long hours and sometimes earning less per hour than teachers who seemed to have more time to do things. The middle managers wondered where it would all end for them, especially when it became clear that the quality improvement movement was here to stay.

However, most of the managers embraced the quality first process. They worked very hard to make it work and generally had good success. A couple of them had more difficulty. They left the organization and went into industry or to other schools. The management situation at FVTC during the early stages can best be described as chaos. When I discussed this with those involved in quality in the private sector, I learned that they encountered similar challenges with middle managers.

Gradually, things got better. Managers learned to support the process and work at developing and using new leadership skills. They realized that we were serious about quality improvement when a volunteer task force was organized to study management and come up with a job description for the manager of the future. Eighteen people volunteered to come up with these new requirements for the college which were later adopted by the TQLC.

Advanced training for managers was something that should have started earlier. This Phase II instructional program began in late 1990. The course designer worked with the task force members to prepare a course in process management. The 36-hour course provided instruction in team building, problem solving, scientific methodology, statistical process control, and customer service. Our managers have been very receptive to learning and practicing these new skills.

If I had to do it again, I would require that all managers and administrators receive this intensive, specialized training early in the process. I would ensure, through closer monitoring by administrators, that the quality first concepts taught during training were used in everyday management. I'd be certain that they learned measurement and costing techniques and became acquainted with scientific methods and the statistical tools. They would receive training in team building, customer service, skills for handling confrontation, and conflict resolution. I'd ask our senior administrators to provide as much support as possible to the managers in their units, and I would continue to reassure these managers that their jobs were secure. I would also ask the board to adopt a job security policy for managers. Hopefully, this would eliminate some of the fear associated with this change in organizational culture and would encourage managers to teach leadership skills to their staff.

Summary

Most quality experts insist about 80 percent of the quality problems in organizations are the direct result of ineffective management. They contend that managers can make the difference in transforming the organization and improving its operation. They say that these same conditions apply to all organizations—manufacturing and service, private sector companies, and public schools.

This does not imply that all educational managers have been ineffective nor does it mean that schools have all been poorly managed. Rather, it means that managers, with proper training and commitment, can transform schools into institutions that foster greater creativity, innovation, and change. At the same time, greater focus on customer service will improve and costs will be reduced.

Perhaps the most important characteristic of this restructuring is the decentralization which occurs. In the transformed environment, curriculum and teaching decisions are usually in the hands of the instructors working hand in hand with their managers and other staff. Service department decisions are usually made by the workers who perform the tasks in concert with their supervisors.

With this comes a new style of management that focuses on leadership by empowerment of others. Managers rely on their coeducators to make the decisions and come up with solutions which affect their daily work. Teams work together to solve unit problems while meeting departmental and school-wide goals.

The long-range goal is the elimination of complacency and mediocrity in schools. While there are countless ways to strive for this, the main emphasis is on respect for the individual team members and commitment to excellence through team action. This concept implies that people involved in education can and want to make a difference.

As a school implements changes to encourage greater involvement by instructors and staff, be cautious. While greater participation is needed, total independence can lead to chaos. Team members will still want and need information, advice, encouragement, and support. Therefore, managers should not hand over the school through administrative abdication. Completely discarding management practices may lead to staff frustration. Each past practice should be evaluated and a determination made whether the processes used can be improved or should be discarded. Active and strong leadership can occur without traditional dictatorships or past heroics. The manager can play a key role in moving teams more and more toward tough decision making and difficult problem solving.

The cultural transformation of schools won't occur all at once. Many managers will be reluctant to turn from their past ways. After all, it is difficult to shed years of traditional management practices. Change will come when people at all levels of the school are willing to take the first steps and convince others to move in the same direction. The number committed to change will multiply as success becomes obvious to the rest. While this is all risky, it is imperative that grass-roots involvement occurs. The needs and challenges facing education are too great to continue with the cosmetic changes advocated by most reforms. Fundamental change from hierarchical systems to horizontal teams led by quality-based managers has the potential to alter the very core of our schools and lead to meaningful improvement.

CHAPTER 7

ROLE OF THE INSTRUCTOR IN THE QUALITY PROCESS

Debate in public education has traditionally looked outside the classroom for answers to improving education. Recent thrusts for improvement have been to hire more specialists, generally using financial resources from categorical aids directed by state or federal projects. The emphasis has been on just about everything except teaching itself. In fact, educational reformers usually portray teachers as being passive recipients of their reform proposals.

More recently, some reformers have begun to realize that in order to ensure continued innovation and greater accountability, changes are needed in the way instructors are hired, trained, certified, and rewarded. They envision schools with more autonomous faculty charged with the responsibility of making their schools better. A major contribution to this thinking came from a report prepared by a task force on teaching funded by the Carnegie Foundation. This new focus on teachers and their role in educational reform is outlined in *A Nation Prepared: Teachers for the 21st Century.*[26]

Using this premise, the major requirement of a quality-based school revolves around the notion that lasting and significant change will not occur in schools unless instructors are directly and actively involved in the planning, development, and implementation of the reforms. In this concept, the ultimate innovator in the school is the teacher. Once teachers are raised in status and become involved in the decision-making process, the rest will follow. Properly motivated teachers can renew themselves and rededicate their careers toward innovation and growth. With the instructor as the focal point for change, new models emerge for restructuring our schools.

The model for change at FVTC is rooted in the quality elements. These elements, found in Appendices E through K, outline conforming requirements which form the basis for excellence in instruction, service, and management of schools. They spell out the critical roles which instructors play in the process. They lay the foundation for new staffing patterns which recognize the individual talents and specialities of faculty and other staff members. The model is based on the premise that giving teachers greater power and responsibility is an important way to improve their performance and their contribution to educating students.

This chapter describes the key roles instructors play when transforming a school into a quality-based environment. It emphasizes the importance of autonomous schools and departments in improving the quality of teaching and learning. It recognizes that it is the individual school, not the comprehensive school district, not the state system, nor the federal department of education that creates an educational model for success.

Some basic concepts require reemphasis to clarify principles that should be uniformly applied in any model that is used. The quality improvement process will work in education if there is:

1. Commitment by top-level administrators and board members.

2. Ongoing education and training for all school personnel.

3. Clarification of roles of all school personnel (including teachers).

4. Empowerment of teachers as a way to increase their decision making and improve their performance.

5. More information sharing with faculty and staff, including data that formerly were distributed only to top administrators.

6. Establishment of school-wide and departmental goals with the application of scientific methods and statistical approaches to determine variability toward process improvement.

7. Appropriate research to use as the foundation for planning and the prevention of defects.

8. New ways of classifying students, school personnel, and external groups, including parents, as customers in the educational enterprise.

9. Greater accountability for each and every process of instruction and management through the establishment of quality elements and measurable conforming requirements.

With these principles in mind, reform in schools will occur when responsibility for learning rests with those most involved, teachers and students. Reforms that place this responsibility in the hands of administrators, legislators, policymakers, or educational experts and consultants simply won't work.

Union Involvement

Teaching unions will not stand in the way of restructuring if the changes advocated are developed with their active involvement. Union members are rethinking their assumptions about the teaching/learning process and how it is organized, and they now agree that they have an active and positive role to play in influencing both the educational environment and the community itself. They are aware of the blurring of jurisdictional lines between managing and teaching, and recognize their need to become proponents of change. Both the American Federation of Teachers (AFT) and the National Education Association (NEA) support changes that occur with the direct involvement of teachers.

Mary Hatwood Futrell, former president of the NEA, says, "We are willing to take risks. But we are willing to do it on our terms, using sound educational research, our own knowledge, our own experience, and time enough to work it out. We realize we may stumble and sometimes fail, but we don't want wholesale failures like we've had in the past."[27]

Albert Shanker, president of the AFT, offers similar advice to administrators who are advocating reform in their schools. He recommends that for schools to change, they must:

• Abandon the idea that there are comprehensive answers that will work in all schools. Successful reform will occur, he believes, on a school-by-school basis, utilizing each staff's strengths in response to local conditions.

• Use the collective knowledge and experience of its teaching staff and its untapped potential to acquire more.[28]

It's obvious that creating schools as centers of renewal and reform will require new policy-making which may be directly influenced by the collective bargaining process. We know that unless there is trust and goodwill, the bargaining process can be used to inhibit change. Therefore, it is imperative to understand that major reform will involve compromises and trade-offs in areas that have traditionally been battlegrounds during negotiations.

With this in mind, school executives and board members must learn to work more closely with unions. They must recognize that giving teachers a voice in the school goes beyond soliciting their suggestions. This involvement by teachers means sharing decisions with them on such crucial matters such as long-range planning, research and development, and cost containment. It's one thing to say to teachers, "You're empowered; you have a right to have a voice." It's another thing to actually give them meaningful influence and control.

Provide unions with an open door by sharing all available management and financial information. Give teachers the education they need to become effective participants in team activities, problem solving, and cooperative management. Approach bargaining issues using problem-solving and conflict resolution techniques rather than adversarial tactics. Formulate economic strategies jointly.

Likewise, union leaders have an obligation to be constructive and helpful, while at the same time representing the interests of their groups. They must dismiss their traditional view of the board and administration as the enemy. They must learn that engaging in cooperative efforts cannot be halfhearted. Most of all, they must realize that new approaches are required because teachers need individual recognition and a sense of being special. These new concepts conflict with traditional bargaining strategies which require that people be treated the same, even though some faculty perform functions that demand more expertise than others.

The ideal union/administration relationship is one in which the two groups are inseparable when it comes to matters of common interest. In this type of setting both groups are comfortable being partners in activities such as strategic planning where information that in the past had been privileged is now shared openly. At the same time, administrators and board members need to recognize that there is nothing inconsistent with collective bargaining and meaningful school change.

This doesn't mean that cooperative relationships will come easily. Patience and reeducation is required, and positive steps must be taken on the part of both the school administration and the union leadership. In some cases it may require that a neutral third party facilitate certain processes.

At the 1989 ASQC Congress in Toronto, a paper titled "The Role of the Union, Management and Consultant in a Total Transformation Effort" was presented with suggestions for both management and unions.

Seven steps were proposed for management to work more effectively with unions. According to the presenters, management should:

1. Understand union concerns regarding changes in the work environment.

2. Develop an understanding of faculty/staff relation laws that may be impacted by the new environment.

3. Recognize that union leaders will need to work out their positions and support for quality in schools.

4. Treat unions as equal partners in the quality improvement effort.

5. Allow for structured changes which permit the unions' active participation on an ongoing basis.

6. Agree on how overlaps between the collective bargaining agreements and the quality approach will be handled.

7. Place priority on discussions regarding job security issues.

The same presenters also described recommendations for unions as equal partners in the quality improvement effort. They contend that the unions should:

1. Develop an understanding of the quality process and learn about issues which could impact on union members.

2. Organize a union steering committee to develop policies and procedures to guide them as an active partner in the process.

3. Define the role of union executive committee members in the quality movement.

4. Work to educate their members regarding all quality process issues which may impact on their contracts.

5. Cooperate with management to develop new possibilities regarding job security for members.

6. Agree with management on how overlaps between the master contract and quality process issues will be handled.

7. Establish networks with other similar unions that are actively involved in quality improvement processes.[29]

Defining Successful Teaching

The first step in strengthening and energizing innovative teaching in the quality-based school is to provide opportunities for teachers to analyze their teaching responsibilities and plan strategies for improvement. This process requires instructors to move away from complete attention to course content and toward behaviors and techniques used by model teachers.

A comprehensive study that attempts this type of analysis was conducted by George A. Baker, III, John E. Roueche, and Rosemary Gillett-Karam. They collected over a million pieces of datum in an effort to determine what makes teachers exemplary. Through interviews, 869 award-winning teachers from community colleges in the United States and Canada gave their opinions and criteria for successful teaching. The teachers' suggestions, together with other insights gained in interviews with their students and their college presidents, are presented in the book *Teaching As Leading: Profiles of Excellence in the Open-Door College*.[30]

What emerged from this extensive study is a description of the teacher as a leader with a reciprocal relationship with students who are followers. In this progressive role, the instructor empowers students much as the effective leader in business and industry empowers his or her workers.

The role and influence of faculty in assisting students in such things as recruitment, orientation, assessment, advisement, placement, and counseling are not identified in the book. Instead, it focuses on the central roles related to the teaching/learning process and examines the critical functions of faculty recruitment, professional development, staff evaluation, and teacher retention.

Teaching As Leading provides the framework to assist school administrators in becoming better predictors of which applicants can and will be successful in teaching students who are attracted to community/technical colleges. Also suggested in the book is an "ideal climate" in which exemplary teachers can thrive and prosper. In this environment, teaching and learning is primary, and faculty and students are no longer at the bottom end of the traditional hierarchical structure. The book also suggests new board policies to permit effective recruitment, selection, development, and reward of teachers. It calls for new roles for faculty in meaningful decision making.

The book introduces the "Teaching As Leading Inventory" (TALI). This inventory classifies instructors into four teaching styles— supporter, theorist, achiever, and influencer. These classifications are integrated with the theories and works of Lewin and Kolb with experiential learning being at the center of the process. The authors concur that all four teaching styles are appropriate and that "situational teaching" is needed to meet the different needs of students and their readiness to learn. Additionally, specific behaviors are suggested to support both directive and supportive styles in a situational teaching/learning environment.[31]

Using this outstanding research about the teaching profession, a group of FVTC faculty and staff met to define quality elements and competencies for the successful teacher at the college. Led by John Hauser, marketing instructor, and Terri Langan, communications instructor, the group used *Teaching As Leading* and other research to establish the exemplary elements for curriculum and instruction and design a system to assist teachers at the college. What emerged were a number of projects and courses which FVTC teams will implement in 1992. The projects and courses will lead to improvements in the instructional process. Facilitators (other instructors) will be available to assist the department teams with their plan for improvement. The general idea is that instructional teams choose one or more of several areas identified through an analysis of the quality elements to work on for improvement in the department. The team, therefore, becomes the agent to design and implement the improvement plan in the department. This concept links the quality process with team goals.

During 1992, all instructors at FVTC will take a special course in teaching in a quality-based school. The primary content will focus on defining teaching competencies, but there will also be instruction in quality awareness, customer service, problem solving, and team building.

Because they are central to defining excellence in teaching and learning, the instructional task force also reviewed and revised the quality elements, especially those for curriculum and instruction. They agreed that through this improvement process, the success model that is emerging at the college is a combination of individual, team, and college-wide goals. All of these goals seek to improve instruction at the college.

The FVTC Teaching Model

Typically, instructors' roles have been identified with their actual contact with students. Work loads and assignments have been organized and calculated accordingly. Teachers in quality-based schools are now assuming roles that reflect new responsibilities, many of which were typically performed by management and technical support staff. Analysis of these new functions and the quality elements were used when developing the teaching model for FVTC.

The quality process model at FVTC uses the seven quality elements identified as follows:

- Human Resources
- Curriculum and Instruction
- Goal Setting
- Use of Technology
- Marketing
- Customer Service
- Management

These elements are the pyramids upon which the quality-based environment is founded at FVTC. While all school personnel have responsibilities for many of these elements, the specific roles of teachers are described below.

Recognizing that competent faculty is key to the learning/teaching process, the quality elements related to *Human Resources* address the responsibilities of both the school and the individual as related to the selection, performance, and evaluation of faculty. Written in measurement terms, requirements specific for teachers are found in each of these areas:

- Qualifications and certification requirements of faculty
- Professional, career, and personal development for each teacher
- Faculty recruitment and affirmative action requirements for the college
- Recognition systems for faculty who meet and exceed goals
- Physical facility requirements for both teachers and students
- Flexibility and creativity of teachers in the learning process
- Characteristics of the caring and enthusiastic teacher
- Teamwork and differentiated roles of faculty

Quality elements were also established for *Curriculum and Instruction* and they are especially directed toward instructors. The conforming requirements state that quality in curriculum and instruction occurs when there is:

- Mastery learning with competency-based approaches in curriculum design
- Adequate course planning for learning following a set standard
- Written course prerequisites
- Pre-assessment processes that identify learning styles
- Criterion-based student measurement systems

- Credit for past learning and other experiences of students
- Multiple-entry/exit delivery systems with opportunities for accelerated learning
- Emphasis on the learning environment itself with a focus on creating enjoyable experiences which are linked to the objectives
- Advisory committee involvement in reviewing the teaching/ learning processes
- Evaluation/audits of instruction and programs
- Articulation with other levels of education
- Class and laboratory management standards
- Techniques for retraining students
- Customized training systems
- Use of current technology by both faculty and students

The planning and budgeting process is an important function of every school. It is defined as the continual process of making decisions in a systematic way, based on review of the past, a look at the future, and analysis of the present. This research and planning system calls for *Goal Setting* as a vital quality element. The FVTC model has requirements for teachers in each of these components. Quality is present in research, planning, and goal setting when there are processes for:

- Determining mission and purpose
- Defining strategic directions
- Identifying and prioritizing program and course needs
- Involving all instructors in the planning process itself
- Integrating planning with budgeting
- Recognizing the need for planning to be continuous and flexible

Effectively merging instructional, administrative, and office information systems enhances the contemporary school. Therefore, the quality element *Use of Current Technology* is required for excellence in both teaching/learning and management of schools. We are using quality in the application of technology when we demonstrate that we are:

- Utilizing computer reports, documents, and electronic communications to assist students and control courses
- Using media and computers to improve teaching and to prepare students for the world of work

- Maintaining computerized student accounting and record systems

- Using technology as a means to individualize instruction and increase flexibility

- Changing roles of teachers from disseminators of information to managers of learning activities which use technology

Since in post-secondary schools marketing involves all levels of personnel, instructors have an important role in both helping to create a positive and favorable image and in the recruitment, retention, and placement of students. The quality element *Marketing* has four requirements that relate specifically to instructors. Faculty are demonstrating quality when they are:

- Defining markets and strategies

- Satisfying external and internal customers

- Creating favorable perceptions of the school

- Performing high school articulation and recruitment activities

The key to the success of any school is defining the customer and meeting and exceeding his or her needs and expectations. This customer-oriented approach is articulated in the quality element *Customer Service*. An organizational team effort is advocated in these requirements. Teachers are providing quality customer service when they:

- Design fun learning activities

- Use customer-friendly systems and programs

- Seek customer feedback

- Handle complaints quickly and positively

Effective management and leadership is crucial to the implementation of the quality process. Therefore, it is essential that quality elements be listed for *Management*. In the new quality-based model, many faculty members are involved in management functions, and several conforming requirements have been defined for those teachers. A teacher is involved in quality management practices when he or she is following processes involved in:

- Developing and accounting for courses and programs

- Scheduling of classes

- Managing classroom activities effectively

- Assigning and monitoring other faculty and teacher aides

- Involving advisory committee in course/program review

- Preparing grant and project proposals

- Conducting team meetings

- Coordinating business/industry contracts

In addition to quality elements which have special focus on the teaching/learning process, the original instructional task force prepared a model for integrated relationships. A description of this model, which was referred to and shown in Figure 3.3, follows.

Relationships With Students

In the quality-based school, teachers are consistent in relationships with all students. Their students know the course expectations (objectives) and understand that they will be evaluated based on defined learning outcomes. Instructors have good communication with students and recognize individual needs and learning differences. They assist students in maximizing learning and in clarifying career goals. They provide an atmosphere where students gain confidence and self-respect.

Instructors establish an environment that is conducive to learning and maximize customer satisfaction as described in Chapter 5. In addition, instructors become role models for the quality process by using the tools and techniques in the learning process. The effect of this all is to give students the expertise to enter, upon graduation, the world of quality and productivity.

Relationships With Peers And Colleagues

In an exemplary school, faculty shares information and materials. A team spirit exists because instructors know each other well. The teachers use good judgment in sharing data and other information about students and other staff members. They are professional in their approach toward people and are respectful of each other. They enhance relationships through cooperative efforts with their coworkers.

They effectively communicate with others, including their managers and administrators. They are accountable and place a special focus on maintaining positive relationships with all people in the school. They seek to develop positive attitudes which foster personal, team, and organizational growth and development.

Relationships With The Community

Besides improving internal relationships, instructors in a quality-based school establish unique relationships with the community. They present a positive image of their school and actively participate in events with business and industry, other schools, and agencies. They constantly update themselves and their programs through meaningful experiences with employers and advisory committee members.

These instructors recognize that it takes special training and techniques to teach in programs that are customized for business and industry. They relate to both management and workers when teaching on site in an industry or business. They understand their important role in representing the school to the community.

Putting It All Together

The quality elements and the integrated model contain the criteria for excellence in the teaching/learning process. All this comes together when there is a constant self-analysis to align the current posture for each program with the goal setting that is a part of the measurement and costing model.

Using scientific methods, problem-solving strategies, and statistical approaches, teams of faculty and staff in each department work together to foster continuous improvement. This process, which is described in the next chapter, provides the monitoring and accountability that is supported by meaningful data as the school moves perpetually forward.

Some Reflections And Thoughts On Application

Nothing significant will happen in schools without the full support of the faculty and staff. Instructors, because of their "front-line" relationships with both students and the community, have special roles to play which are most significant.

For some reason, I expected that most of our teachers would be opposed to the whole idea of incorporating a formal quality improvement process into education. What a pleasant surprise it was to see their general acceptance of the concepts! Of course there were some who felt that this was an administrative ploy to reduce costs and make teachers more accountable. They were suspicious from the start and were slow to jump on the quality bandwagon. Some never will.

I was pleased when the union leaders in the school embraced the idea. They welcomed the opportunity to be involved in more decision making, and they appreciated efforts to improve communications with management. They were grateful for data and information which were made available to them for the first time.

One of the more pleasant and worthwhile efforts we began as a part of the quality effort was the establishment of monthly luncheon meetings involving the executives of both unions and the senior administrators of the college. The quality coordinator attends and there is an open agenda format—any issue is fair game for discussion. The school provides lunch and the meeting is held on the same day as the college board meeting. There are usually questions about upcoming board agenda items and several questions and concerns about other things happening in school. Sometimes there are complaints. Often there are mutual compliments. We try to avoid anything related to the negotiation process.

This monthly event has opened the door for greater communications. It has given senior school executives an appreciation of the concerns and issues troubling faculty and staff. Usually, those concerns or issues are the result of poor communications. They are usually cleared up immediately, but sometimes there are issues which require follow-up and investigation.

FVTC faculty have always been willing to adjust to change, and their acceptance of the quality process with all its transformational impacts wasn't much different. I was amazed, however, to see the faculty leaders' willingness to look at major issues, some of which I thought were "untouchable." For example, following a college study conducted by the faculty union head and one of our school managers on the "time" issue, I was encouraged to see recommendations related to the possibility of accepting changing roles for faculty, together with new systems of compensation. It became apparent to me that the union leaders were most willing to assist in solving major problems when given the chance. Both of our current union executives, Ron Toshner, president of the Faculty Association, and Yvonne Matz, president of the Educational Support Staff Association, outline their thoughts and impressions of the quality process at FVTC in Appendix D.

With this spirit of cooperation and atmosphere receptive to change, I believe that new staffing models will emerge. The blur between what managers do and what faculty accept as new responsibilities will cause radical changes not only in how teachers and managers relate to one another but also in the way the school is structured.

There may be a new organization that narrows the gaps between management and faculty/staff. There may be new staffing and organizational structures with new compensation plans for both managers and instructors. Such radical changes are now possible at

FVTC. What's especially significant is that both the union and management agree that teaching responsibilities and definitions of instructional roles need reexamination. Since some instructors will have varying roles and other responsibilities besides teaching that are related to their special talents and interests, we will need to change the ways responsibilities are given to and carried out by managers. If managers are leaders who work with teams of teachers by empowering them and giving greater responsibilities, then other aspects of teacher functions and those of their managers may require change.

These new, differentiated structures may lead to fewer managers who work closely with teachers to operate autonomous work units without a lot of supervision and interference. Examples of teachers who have accepted these new roles and managers who have become this type of leader are emerging at the college. Programs and services have been enhanced by these cooperative arrangements and the prospect for continued success is promising.

Many teachers at the college have tried innovative approaches and accepted new responsibilities involving:

- Curriculum design

- Accelerated learning

- Counseling and advisement

- Management and coordination

- Use of interactive technology

- Team building

- Research and development

- Marketing, recruitment, and placement of graduates

Changes in roles and functions will happen and new models will emerge if there is an atmosphere of trust and communication. This takes time and patience.

In my opinion, the quality process model at FVTC is one mechanism which has the potential to make it happen.

Summary

Advocates of educational reform are beginning to realize that lasting and significant change will not occur without direct and active involvement by teachers. They feel that to ensure continued innovation and greater accountability, changes are needed in the way teachers are hired, trained, certified, and rewarded. The ideal school has autonomous faculty charged with the responsibility of making their schools more effective.

The FVTC quality improvement model is based on the establishment of quality elements, each of which has a series of criteria called conforming requirements. At FVTC there are seven sets of elements, all of which establish goals of excellence. The elements and their requirements are established in cooperation with the faculty and staff. They are based on customer expectations with a goal of constantly meeting or exceeding those expectations. Teachers have special requirements in each of the elements, particularly in "curriculum and instruction."

This chapter reinforces the principles which will make the quality process work in an educational setting. The key concepts are similar to those found in business and industry because they call for decision making at the level closest to the customer and focus on prevention rather than inspection.

Building effective relationships with instructors is enhanced by the recognition that teaching unions have been receptive to the concepts of quality improvement. This chapter stresses the importance of both management and unions agreeing that they are equal partners in fostering the change process that occurs when implementing quality improvement systems. New school structures will call for different roles and responsibilities for faculty and a blurring of jurisdictional lines between managing and teaching. Ideas and suggestions for improving relationships between management and unions are presented.

This chapter also shows efforts at FVTC to describe successful teaching and define teacher competencies. Several insights were incorporated from research reported in the book *Teaching As Leading: Profiles of Excellence in the Open-Door College*. The authors present excellent ideas for improving the recruitment, hiring, training, and evaluation of instructors.

Also described in this chapter are the efforts of two instructor task forces active at FVTC. The original task force developed an integrated relationships' framework which became the basis for discussion during the initial faculty training program. Another group of faculty/staff designed several "teaching excellence" projects and a course that focuses on improving the roles and effectiveness of teachers. The team will become the agent to incorporate the preferred improvement plan in each department. The concept links the quality process with team goals.

The chapter closes with some reflections and thoughts on the future of the instructional process at FVTC.

CHAPTER 8

APPROACHES TO MEASURING AND COSTING QUALITY IN EDUCATION

- Can we describe, judge, and improve the effectiveness of schools?

- Can we correctly and concisely measure and control the variances found in the processes common to education?

- Can quality in education be looked at in financial terms as it is in business and industry?

- Are process management approaches useful for measurement and improvement in education?

These important questions are being considered as school critics, with increasing frequency, demand reform and accountability in education. Educators must look for answers, for no matter how good they feel our schools have been, they must become better to meet the educational needs of our fast-changing, technological world. Responsibility for our nation's economic well-being is being placed squarely in the realm of education and calls for school change are more prevalent than ever before. Many reformers are insisting that there be a complete overhaul of the educational system. These demands are coming from people external to schools—parents, citizens, and legislators, rather than from the educational establishment—teachers, administrators, and graduate school professors. While I agree that new systems of accountability are needed in education, I believe they should be designed by educators themselves.

Schools, by their very nature, are continually involved in measurement and evaluation, whether it be testing the success of students, measuring the competence of teachers and staff, or assessing the need for improvement. Some of these practices need renewal and the public is asking for different methods of assessment to replace those thought to be archaic and outmoded. Since education is critical to our nation's future, we can no longer maintain the status quo. We must turn to business practices and techniques that include the use of process management and statistical approaches to accountability.

Somewhere between traditional school operation and radical reform lies the answer to improvement of our schools. The quality improvement process provides the mechanism, I believe, for the meaningful change which is required. While these changes should be fostered by educators themselves, private sector techniques of management, measurement, and costing can be applied. This chapter gives the reader a global reference to process management and the use of statistical approaches in education. It is not intended to be a text on the use of scientific methodology and the application of statistical process control tools. That information can be found in numerous other books. Rather, this chapter suggests using basic measurement techniques and determining cost reductions that result from the quality process in education.

Education—A Service Industry

Before applying process management techniques to a service organization, such as a school, it's necessary to understand the unique nature and characteristics of services. Unfortunately, many people assume that the statistical approaches that have been used successfully in manufacturing can be applied the same way to any and all service operations. Dr. A. C. Rosander, who has over 45 years of experience in probability sampling, quality control, and statistical analysis and is the recipient of the 1984 Howard Jones Award from the Quality Management Division of ASQC, states that this type of thinking "puts service quality control in a straitjacket." He argues that "willy nilly attempts at applying manufacturing approaches to service organizations limits the application, does not recognize that services are not the same as physical products, does not acknowledge the significant differences in the quality functions in different service industries, ignores many techniques which can be used in services but are not used in manufacturing, and refuses to consider the fact that services are dominated by subjective human elements and not by precise physical measurements."[32]

In his book *The Quest for Quality in Services*, Rosander contends that while measurement can be applied to service operations, services cannot be measured in the same sense that physical products are. He points to the unique characteristics of service industries that can be summarized as:

- Face-to-face relations between the provider and the customer

- Many people involved in the process

- Many money transactions

- Large masses of paper generated

- Human failure, equipment failure, or both

- No mechanical controls over variation, as there are in factories

- Computer systems which require special controls over input data and the computer program itself

- Process control techniques which may be used to improve quality

He further contends that in service, "the only level we want to set for errors, mistakes, and blunders is zero. The only level we want for wasted time is zero. We should not set an acceptable level for discourtesy, rudeness, indifference, or surliness." He also argues that service industries are not trying to stabilize a certain dimension so that it falls within tolerances. Instead of maintaining a certain level, he believes that service industries want to eliminate poor quality completely.[33]

In spite of their unique characteristics, services have many features which can be measured. To begin with, specifications can be written for observable things. Most studies list three major determinants of the quality of services: (1) behavior, (2) attitudes, and (3) appearance. These things can be observed and can be measured even though, in most cases, they are under the control of the immediate provider. Because of this and unlike manufacturing, the ratios which define poor quality may not fit the 85-15 (manager/provider) responsibility level that experts usually apply. Managers in schools have responsibility for selecting the right person for a position, providing proper training, establishing a customer-service atmosphere, and assisting the provider (teacher, support staff, technician), but the providers of the services similarly must accept responsibility for their attitudes, behavior, and appearance.

Statistical Approaches

At the heart of quality improvement is the use of systematic ways for teams to address problems in processes. This involves scientific approaches, including the use of statistical tools. Educational leaders are sometimes apprehensive about this because most have not received advanced training in statistics. It is essential, however, that educational managers know and apply elementary statistics so that variability in processes can be detected, controlled, reduced, and prevented. These skills, typically learned in graduate school, include learning the measures of central tendency (mean, mode, median), the use of ranges, and knowledge of variation through the determination of standard deviations from the mean. In graduate research application courses, educators are taught to use calculations which may involve applying statistical formulae. These applications, together with the use of scientific method, are, in this book, grouped under the broad category of process management. Used properly, process management, which includes scientific methodology, the use of statistical tools, and the application of good data to decision making, can be helpful in education.

Statistics are just a descriptive index of how we're doing. They tell us which areas are doing fine and which require changes. They help us monitor and improve our services to our internal and external customers. We cannot set goals in education without knowing how the processes are doing now. Without measuring, we can't tell if we're getting better or not. Statistics help us do this and we get the numbers for statistical analysis through measurement.

We can't measure everything, so we have to be selective. The key is to choose problems to solve which can significantly improve the operations and services of the school and then determine what measurements will assist in monitoring the proposed solutions. To be meaningful, measurements must be valid and reliable. Our measurements have validity when they actually measure what they're supposed to. They have reliability when they are precise, accurate, and consistent.

There will always be a need for careful analysis of processes and systems to reveal the problems involving quality in schools. Educators can measure mistakes, delays, accidents, and other behavior which influence quality, productivity, and efficiency of operations. They can analyze wasted time, faulty teaching schedules, poor student schedules, inadequate working conditions, conflicts between management and teachers, inefficient methods, poor equipment operations, and the lack of communication. They can calculate clerical mistakes, judgment errors, and other deviations by technicians in service departments. Likewise, observable conditions and employee behavior traits and attitudes can be measured. In addition, it's possible for instructors to use statistical analysis to improve processes in the various teaching/learning systems which they employ.

Information systems are an important part of this. Data can be used to solve existing problems, to reveal new problems, and to point to processes which may create future problems. A critical factor is the proper preparation and analysis of written processes and procedures that are used in data collection. Decisions are no better than the data on which they are based. Therefore, special care must be taken to ensure that proper techniques and practices are used in data collection. Despite the potential of faulty data, though, it is much better to operate a school by making decisions based on data rather than on hunches or intuition.

Variation

But measurements alone are not enough. It's also important to analyze what the measurements tell us about a process. While service institutions such as schools are usually not trying to stabilize dimensions so they fall within certain levels, it is often important to know how our processes vary. It is useful, therefore, to understand and correctly interpret variation in the products and services of schools.

As stated earlier, decisions are often based on the interpretation of patterns of variation among available data. Educational managers must therefore understand basic statistical concepts to interpret variation. They must be able to determine whether the patterns indicate a trend or random variation. They must understand that indicators of performance of any process or system should be identified and measured because these characteristics may vary over time and in different situations. They must also recognize and take steps to reduce common and special causes of variation:

> **Common-cause variation**—Inherent variation in a process or system that affects everything and everyone. Since it is always present, its origin can usually be traced to an element of the system that only management can correct.

> **Special-cause variation**—Causes that are nonrandom patterns so are not always part of the process and do not affect everything and everyone. They are intermittent, unpredictable, and unstable and may be signaled by points beyond defined control limits.

A process that has only common-cause variation affecting the outcomes is a stable process because the cause system for variation remains relatively constant over time. Such variation is predictable within statistically established limits. When special-cause variation occurs in the process, it is an unstable process. Removing special causes brings the process into statistical control.

Understanding and controlling variations is a subject at the very heart of Deming's theories. He contends that the goal is to reduce variation as much as possible. One approach is to standardize processes so that everyone is using the same procedures, materials, and equipment. Another is to study the process, look for potential sources of variation, and collect data. Elimination of special-cause variation is the first step. Then comes the more difficult job of trying to eliminate common-cause variation.

The methodology of gathering and analyzing data and determining what measurements tell about processes is statistical process control (SPC). This shows us graphically what variation is occurring. The charts indicate whether variation in a process is dominated by common or special causes. They show the measurement of a certain process characteristic (waste or error rate) with data plotted in time order. Data are plotted on a chart and through the use of basic statistics, average and range or percent is shown. The center line on the chart is the average or mean of the data. Upper and lower control limits are then calculated by determining the standard deviation from the average. Points outside the upper and lower control limits (+ or - three standard deviations) are indications of the existence of special causes. Those within the control limits are common causes.

The graphic way to show common-cause variation is the normal or bell-shaped curve. In this curve, most things are in the middle with fewer things on both ends. It is symmetric and has an average precisely in the middle. In the normal curve, we know that approximately 68 percent of the total area falls within plus or minus one standard deviation from the exact middle. We also know that 96 percent of the total area falls within plus or minus two standard deviations from the exact middle. The other four percent of variation occurs within the third standard deviation on either end of the normal curve.

Special-cause variation changes the pattern of the normal curve. When abnormal things happen, it is reflected in the distribution curve. The immediate objective is to determine if there are special causes and then decide how to eliminate them. Once special-cause variation is gone, the more difficult job of reducing common-cause variation can begin.

So far we have talked about characteristics that we can measure and attach a value. Each characteristic has a critical dimension and we count how often something happens, how much time something takes, or the quantity of something. This type of data are variable data.

While variable data have an infinite number of values, another type, attribute data, can be sorted into only two categories (yes/no, pass/fail, good/bad). When we group units into one category or the other and then count them, we are working with attribute data. These types of datum are less expensive to collect and quicker to obtain than variable data. There are several types of attribute charts and they are all useful in education.

As will be shown later in this chapter, special- and common-cause variation can be shown on statistical control charts. These charts have two lines, control limits, that are calculated from measurements taken on the process. Control charts monitor processes and signal patterns which require the identification of special causes. The goal is to reach statistical control or stability with respect to the characteristic being measured.

There are several applications of variation analysis and the use of control charts in education. Decisions need to be made to modify equipment, to adjust enrollment forecasts, to change existing inventory processes, to study absences, to monitor student complaints, and to analyze budget forecasts. Educational leaders making those decisions need basic skills of statistical analysis and a knowledge of patterns of variation, together with an understanding of common and special causes. More importantly, they need to know when to make the fundamental changes necessary to improve quality in our schools.

While control charts are powerful, they must be used on a continual basis and monitored perpetually. It is essential that they are carefully used in order to be credible. This takes time and diligence. As a result, control charts are used sparingly when compared with other statistical tools.

Besides understanding variation and knowing how to use and interpret control charts, educational managers must learn the basic skills of problem solving. They must bring about cultural change in schools and recognize the benefits of having people work together in teams. Managers should empower their team members to identify processes that are creating trouble and to oversee the use of problem-solving skills to eliminate the problems. They assist teams in planning and managing projects and in improving processes through scientific tools and methods. They help team members get reeducated and search for those who should receive specialized training to provide technical assistance to the rest of the team. In summary, educational managers become leaders in enabling team members to use tools, techniques, and attitudes that will make teamwork successful in school.

The Basic Strategies And Tools

Educators should learn to use and interpret the basic strategies that are most frequently applied to quality improvement. They should also become acquainted with the scientific methods which are more common to business and industry. Peter R. Scholtes, in the Joiner Publication *The Team Handbook,* lists four strategies for using scientific methods to help teams that are new to quality improvement:

1. **Collect Meaningful Data**—Perhaps the single most important strategy is to gather reliable data. Data must be free of measurement errors and suited to its purpose. This requires knowing exactly why data are collected and ensuring that they are appropriate to the problem at hand.

2. **Identify Root Causes**—Since the goal is to solve problems permanently, it is essential to get at the underlying or root cause of the problem. To do this, analyze each option until all team members are convinced that the real cause has been identified.

3. **Develop Appropriate Solutions**—Even though team members may think they know the cause of the problem beforehand, it is essential to support hunches with meaningful data. This strategy requires the team to define the goals and gather data on a variety of alternatives.

4. **Plan and Make Changes**—There is no substitute for careful planning. This strategy calls for team members to look ahead, anticipate needs and training requirements, and speculate on possible problems which may come up.[34]

Once these strategies are accepted and used, there are several problem-solving techniques and tools available for improving processes in the school setting. The techniques are brainstorming, flowcharting, and cause and effect diagramming. The basic tools are check sheets, histograms, Pareto charts, scatter diagrams, and control charts. Samples of these tools are found in the case studies toward the end of this chapter. These tools help solve chronic problems, but before they are used, it is necessary to determine how they fit into the total problem-solving activity.

Brainstorming techniques may be used to choose a problem, to study and gather input on its causes, and to flowchart the process. Brainstorming enhances group participation and encourages creativity and new ideas. It is a group problem-solving method that taps people's creative ability to select, define, and solve problems. It allows people to feel comfortable contributing to the group and building trust in each other. During brainstorming, a flowchart is developed that outlines the normal process of the problem which has been identified. The flowchart gives everyone an understanding of how the process works. An example of a flowchart which has been used in education is found on page 103.

A team member facilitates the brainstorming process. He or she exercises enough control over the group to keep it on track while at the same time encouraging total participation by team members. Everyone takes a turn to express an idea which is recorded. Wild ideas are encouraged and criticism of ideas is not allowed.

Since the list of ideas becomes a mixed-up array of thoughts, some organization is required. This may be accomplished with a cause and effect diagram. This diagram shows pictorially how the ideas from brainstorming relate to one another. It arranges disjointed ideas into a logical order so they can be better organized. The cause and effect diagram, sometimes called an Ishikawa or "fish bone" diagram, helps to look at ideas, establish relationships, and examine factors that may influence a given process or evaluation.[35] Examples of cause and effect diagrams that have been used in education are found on pages 102 and 111.

Collect Data And Chart Results

After the process is flowcharted and the cause and effect diagram is constructed, the team decides how to attack the problem, what the problem-solving goals should be, and what data are needed. Then a plan is established to collect the data and chart the results.

To ensure collection of the correct data, clarify the purpose for which data are to be collected. Using carefully written operational definitions, the data are then collected and used to provide a basis for action or change. The data will help identify which defects are most prevalent and which factors are causing defects.

Once the team decides on the type of data needed, the next step is to choose the sampling technique. Types of samples desired, the frequency of their collection, and the sampling methods to be used must be determined. All team members should have an awareness of possible errors in measurement and know how to keep errors to a minimum. The manager or team leader assists by providing instruction in correct measurement techniques. The team should know that different readings may result from using different measurement instruments and/or from different people reading and interpreting the data. They should be encouraged to use existing reports to assist in determining the kinds of defects which are occurring. However, it is important to ensure that the data are appropriate and based on a clear operational definition. Often times the use of data that is collected for state reports or for other purposes is not appropriate for measurement purposes.

A data sheet or check sheet is then used to gather the information desired. These forms organize the data in a meaningful way. While there are several examples of check sheets that may be useful in education, any form is acceptable as long as it provides an organized approach to tally the data. After the information is collected, decide how to arrange the data. Since data are collected in various forms, different formats may be used to arrange and display the data. Two of these, histograms and Pareto charts, are the most popular.

A histogram is used to identify overall tendencies. It is a simple graph with bars. Within a frequency table, data is sequenced and displayed on a graph that shows the shape of distribution of the data. A histogram is built by creating a frequency distribution of the collected data. After the frequency distribution is prepared, a graph is drawn with class intervals on the horizontal axis. The vertical axis shows the sum of the observations or calculations within each class interval. Once drawn, the histogram shows the shape of the distribution. Sometimes the histogram shows a symmetrical or normal distribution (normal curve) where most of the instances occur in the middle, with a fairly equal distribution on both sides. Other distributions that may merge on a histogram include the bimodal pattern, characterized by two separate and distinct groupings of data; skewed patterns which have data grouped abnormally to the right or left; and random patterns, where no distinct data groupings occur.

A Pareto chart is a bar graph that shows the frequency of problems in decreasing order of significance. This chart indicates which problem occurs most frequently and should, therefore, be handled first. The Pareto chart is sometimes described as a way to sort out the "vital few" from the "trivial many." It is helpful because it identifies the major problems in descending order. Besides displaying bars in descending order of frequency from left to right, the chart features an axis to show percentages. The percentage for each additional bar is added to reflect 100 percent of all cases. Examples of Pareto charts which have been used in education are found on pages 108 and 109.

Various sampling techniques and other types of charts are used to gather data and display information. The method used is influenced by the process being examined and the sophistication of the observer and charter. Whenever possible, data should be collected by the person who is closest to the activity because that person can also initiate corrective action in real time. Using check sheets, calculators, computers, and existing data, the person responsible for the activity looks at the data and, in cooperation with his or her manager, interprets the information in an effort to improve the process. The person in charge of the process is usually the best equipped to identify special causes of variation and then eliminate them.

Control Charts

Control charts are graphic illustrations of a process or attribute, showing plotted values with statistically determined central lines and upper and lower control limits. They may be used to determine whether the process has been operating within acceptable limits. In that context, they can provide reliable information upon which appropriate decisions can be made. These variable charts provide information that is valuable in reducing variation through careful analysis of the items that are statistically "out of control." Both variable and attribute control charts may lead to improved quality and productivity because the data help to identify special causes that may be eliminated or that may lead to changes in the process itself.

Walter A. Shewhart, a statistician for Bell Laboratories, developed the techniques to bring processes into "statistical control." He defined the limits of variation through the setting of acceptable highs and lows. As stated earlier, statistical process control (SPC) is the entire process of measuring, charting, and recognizing when to act and when to leave alone. Using SPC, performance can be measured both before and after corrective action has been taken. Since the goal in education is to improve the quality of instruction and services, we must have stable processes because only then can there be confidence in the level of quality. Statistical methods of quality control provide a way to picture and control quality. The greatest value of these techniques comes from using them continuously to control quality. Therefore, to be effective they must become a way of life.[36]

When using SPC, charts are generated from the information that is gathered and these variable data show if the process meets or exceeds the conforming requirements. The charts point out the defects that need to be reduced or eliminated and they permit analysis of the variation in a dimension configured by all parts of the total process. The charts become communication tools that signal when to act and when to leave the process alone.

Control charts are graphic and numeric communication tools. They point out special causes that need to be controlled to improve the process. They show common-cause variation which may be controlled and lead to significant process improvement. School managers, skilled in using and interpreting control charts and other tools, can assist others in the corrective process by using data, not guesswork, to identify needed action.

The design and analysis of control charts does not require advanced statistics; however, before the charts are used, a review of SPC is needed. There are several books available that have illustrations and explanations of statistical techniques used in establishing limits on control charts.

One excellent resource is the Transformation of American Industry Training System which was developed to increase the capacity of our nation's community colleges for helping industry improve quality. The training materials were developed especially for use in business and industry, but they may also be appropriate for educational managers who are learning the basic techniques of SPC.[37]

Control charts perform many functions which will help schools improve their quality. While their basic purpose is to measure quality progress and improvement and point out trouble areas, they may also be used as a history of processes in education. They may be used as presentation and information systems. Most of all, they display variability by showing special causes and pointing out our common causes which, if controlled effectively, can lead to significant improvement. Control charts give school managers objective statistical information which will help in decision making. Such an information system is needed to ensure that problems are solved analytically, goals are attained, and results are monitored. Some examples of control charts which have been used in education are found on pages 106 and 107.

Goal Setting

Two levels of goals are used in the quality/measurement process in education. First, there are global goals which are the main targets from which operational plans are developed. These goals point to the conforming requirements found in the school's quality elements (measures of excellence). Another level of measurement comes from problem-solving activities that are ongoing in the various school departments or work units. Goals are established and are based on the various problems that are being attacked. The foremost goal should always be continued improvement and the quality process provides the vehicle to make this happen.

As the umbrella over this all, the school should list long-range goals and objectives in its strategic plan. These goals and the mission statement form the basis for the existence and operation of the institution. The mission and purpose, the long-range goals, and the quality elements provide the overall direction for the staff. The quality elements are influenced by the school's goals, mission, and purpose, and they form the organizational targets for the quality improvement process. The 16-step quality process model provides the "how" to facilitate this all. Conforming requirements, which are established for each of the elements, become the basis for measurement and costing that determine whether improvement is occurring in the organization. Using problem-solving and statistical approaches, the staff in the work units establish and measure their unique goals.

All school personnel need to be familiar with the school's mission, purpose, long-range goals, and quality elements. Don't assume that staff know these just because they are written in handbooks, policies, and other publications. A formal process to familiarize staff with the philosophical foundation is required.

Department goal setting should emphasize the methods or processes used to meet customers' needs. According to Deming, the establishment of team objectives is composed of these four subprocesses:

- identify customer needs

- determine sources of improvement

- identify who can help accomplish improvement

- develop mutual objectives[38]

Goal setting is, therefore, an important part of the planning process in schools and problems will probably occur if goals are set and measured in isolation from the total planning processes of the organization.

Process Management

Many administrators are using new methods to operate their schools, including the business approaches described in this book. Teachers and other staff are asked to contribute their knowledge and expertise to improve processes and provide exceptional customer service. The changes are deliberate, however, and schools are just beginning new ways to do business. All this change requires managers who know how to monitor, control, and constantly improve processes. This "process management" emphasizes improvement by using methods that focus on quality instead of numerical goals and outcomes. This is done using scientific methods to solve problems and make needed improvements.

Process management is used at FVTC in three major areas, summarized as follows:

School-Wide Measurement and Costing

These activities occur across the school in a cyclical process that is integrated with overall planning and resource allocation. The overall measurement criteria are a set of quality elements that have a list of conforming requirements and a series of measurement strategies. The elements are used throughout the organization for self-assessment and for audits conducted by people external to the school. They are linked to the planning process since school departments use them as a basis for goal setting, problem solving, and measurement. They can be thought of as "umbrella" criteria of school excellence. School-wide costing of poor quality occurs by determining the costs associated with not conforming to the requirements. Figure 8.1 shows this school-wide measurement and costing model. It contains seven main activities that lead to the identification and selection of problems, the measurement and costing of them, and the establishment of institutional and departmental goals.

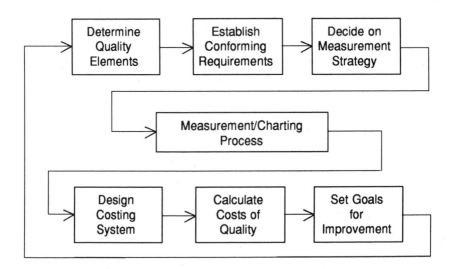

Figure 8.1 – The Cyclical Process of Goal Setting, Measuring, and Costing Quality

School-Wide Process Improvement Projects

These are centralized problem-solving projects that focus on problems that cross department boundaries. They are a part of a larger effort to transform a school and usually will have direct impact on external customers. Projects are selected when several people in the school feel there is an important area to study and there is the potential to greatly improve services and realize significant financial savings. Typically, five or six people from different personnel levels are selected to be on the project team and they are assisted by a group of advisors who have expertise to help the team. A charge is given to the team and this forms the basis for the team to write the mission statement and determine the goals for the project.

Department Problem-Solving Projects

These projects are selected by work unit or department teams. They are chosen following an analysis of the various recurring problems in obvious need of correction. The solution of these problems is under the control of the team itself and, as a result, will probably have immediate impact on the overall operation of the department. Most quality experts agree that real quality improvement occurs at this level of the organization when teams use appropriate problem-solving techniques to foster continued and lasting improvement. With proper training, a group of people who pool their skills can tackle complex and chronic problems and come up with permanent solutions. When this happens on a regular basis, the department is practicing real quality improvement.

Monitoring The Process

In education, some standards of excellence are needed. They are used as the basis for self-analysis during reviews and audits by teams external to the school. If carefully selected and applied, they can be ongoing standards which are used during regional and national accreditation reviews for evaluation purposes. As stated earlier, these standards of excellence at FVTC are called quality elements.

The elements serve as the basis for school-wide goal setting, measurement, and costing. They target the global aspects of the college and their selection and use is based on input by faculty and staff. The standards show how individuals contribute to educational excellence, the conditions under which the activity is performed, and the way the performance is measured.

Seven quality elements evolved during the first few years of the quality improvement process. The elements are shown in Appendices E through K with their conforming requirements, their measurement strategies, and their costs of nonconformance (costs that occur when they are not met). Complete descriptions of these elements and a further explanation of their use are found in the *Fox Valley Technical College Quality Elements Manual* which was published in February 1991.[39] They remain under constant review by the faculty and staff and are changed as required. The seven elements are:

Human Resources—personnel, environment, and organizational climate criteria which serve as standards of excellence

Curriculum and Instruction—curriculum and evaluation standards and guidelines that establish the roles of students and faculty in the instructional process

Goal Setting—standards of excellence for the design and implementation of operational and college-wide plans which, linked to the budget, form the basis for institutional renewal and growth

Technology—standards for the effective use of technology, including computers, media, and other types of telecommunications, that are integrated into an up-to-date information system

Marketing—criteria for all activities that align the mission, goals, and objectives with communications to external and internal publics that are timely and targeted while projecting a positive school image

Customer Service—standards of excellence for dealing with external and internal customers to meet and exceed their individual needs

Management—standards of excellence in providing leadership to the implementation and enhancement of the quality improvement process

These standards of excellence are continuously used as monitors. While they have varying degrees of measurement validity and reliability, they are all used as indicators of improvement at the college. The general goal is to increase their effectiveness through constant use and ongoing improvement of the conforming requirements. Various strategies are used in the ongoing monitoring system at FVTC. The measurement plan for the college for the next three years is found in Appendix L. A brief summary of each measurement strategy is included.

Instructional Audits

Conducted by an outside team of experts from business, industry, and other schools, instructional audits provide a review of instructional programs. A comprehensive audit of each program is conducted at least once every seven years. A computerized "mini-audit" is conducted annually and the results may prompt a comprehensive audit as needed prior to the normal sequence.

Service Unit Audits

Audits of all service units of the college are conducted to examine technical and support service departments such as Student Services,

Human Resources, and Food Service. These departments are evaluated every five years by people from business and industry.

Accreditation Reviews

Accreditation reviews involve an intensive self-evaluation and analysis completed at intervals of five to ten years, depending on the conditions reported in the prior accreditation visit. The quality process, together with the goal setting, measuring, and costing activities, becomes the basis for the self-evaluation study for accreditation reviews. Properly applied, the quality elements can provide an ongoing analysis of school improvement.

Student Satisfaction Surveys

Student satisfaction surveys are conducted to find out how well the school is meeting students' needs. At FVTC, students can evaluate each course. In addition, a regular campus-wide student satisfaction survey is conducted. Results are reported to both students and staff. At graduation, students complete an exit survey and these results are analyzed and reported.

Organizational Climate Surveys

All college employees regularly complete an organizational climate survey that focuses on the quality of services provided by managers as well as the work environment of the school. An analysis of this data becomes the vehicle for promoting greater communication between employees and their managers and for taking action as needed to improve problem areas.

Employer Satisfaction Surveys

Employers of FVTC graduates provide feedback concerning the competence and attitudes of the graduates. This annual survey notes factors that are important to improvement of the instruction and operations of the school.

Graduate Placement Surveys

Conducted six months after graduation, an annual survey tracks graduates' success in jobs. Placement statistics, starting salaries, and other information about jobs held are gathered and analyzed for each instructional program. Three-year and five-year follow-up surveys measure graduate placement over longer periods.

Regional Studies

Surveys of community residents, businesses, and high school students are conducted in each of five regional areas served by the college. Local needs for specific courses, course times, and formats are assessed in each region. A service plan is developed for each region and distributed throughout the region.

Perception Surveys

Perception surveys track the college's image in the community. These surveys, which are conducted every three years, explore how the overall quality of the college, its students, and its programs of study are perceived by people in the communities.

Indicators of District Health

A monthly report made available to the FVTC Board and the college staff graphically defines indicators that may be used to assess improvement of the school. Comparative three-year data related to applications, enrollments, withdrawals, graduations, and other demographic information about the college and its customers are included in this report, called Indicators of District Health. Figure 8.2 is an illustration of this type of report.

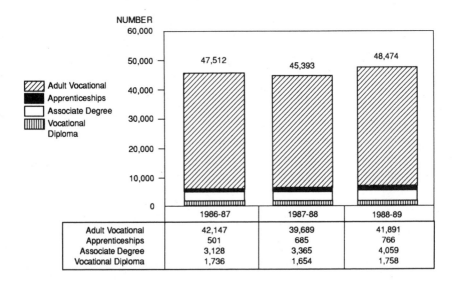

	1986-87	1987-88	1988-89
Adult Vocational	42,147	39,689	41,891
Apprenticeships	501	685	766
Associate Degree	3,128	3,365	4,059
Vocational Diploma	1,736	1,654	1,758

Figure 8.2 – Indicators of District Health (Head Count)

Source: FVTC Summary by Program (Ungraded)

Other Reports and Surveys

Numerous other reports, including attendance records, accident reports, advisory committee minutes, and budget reviews, are used as a part of the measurement and reporting strategy. There are also numerous ad hoc surveys of staff, students, and employers. In addition, continuous process improvement (CPI) reports and comments received in suggestion boxes are used as a means for students, faculty, and staff to report problems and make suggestions.

Fox Valley Case Studies

To illustrate the application of process management and the use of scientific methods in education, two case studies are presented. They are both actual reports of problem-solving activities that included scientific techniques and the use of basic tools of collection and measurement. The first study involves a project related to cafeteria sales on the FVTC Oshkosh campus. The investigation was conducted by Oshkosh campus staff under the leadership of Catherine Zimmerman, campus administrator.[40] The second is a report of a study conducted by Virgil Noordyk, dean of the Technical Division, to determine which technical programs were revenue-producing during the summer months and which were not.[41]

MEASUREMENT PROJECT: Determine Sales Factors Which Impact Most on Income of Oshkosh Campus Cafeteria

The Oshkosh branch campus cafeteria provides food services to the students and staff. The cafeteria offers breakfast and lunch each day that school is in session for approximately 300 students and a staff of 35. The cafeteria also exists to provide training facilities for a maximum of 12 food service students. Because of this, the cafeteria operations are driven by instructional needs and this has created the following problems:

1. The menu is determined by the curriculum; therefore, items prepared are not always what is popular for a school cafeteria.

2. The food service students are attending other classes when meals are served and the area is cleaned; therefore, student labor must be supplemented with paid staff.

3. The students, in a training mode, waste more food than in a regular food service operation.

4. Food service faculty were hired because of their food preparation expertise and may not have strong business backgrounds.

Zimmerman conducted this study because the cafeteria has been losing money annually. In 1989-90, it lost $6,347. She hypothesized that there were several causes of the problem. To begin with, the pool of customers is limited because the campus is small. Therefore, the operation cannot take advantage of cost savings by purchasing food in large quantities. In addition, the staff hired to supplement the student labor are paid union scale wages and receive fringe benefits. These costs are considerably higher than private sector food service operations. Another factor that increases costs relates to the food that is prepared. Usually, more food is produced than sold and this results in considerable waste. All these factors are outlined in a Cause and Effect Diagram shown in Figure 8.3. The diagram organizes the problem areas in a systematic way and assists in determining which data to collect and how to proceed.

Next, a flowchart shows the food preparation and sales sequence. This chart is shown in Figure 8.4. It documents the sequence developed to ensure that all staff become familiar with the process.

Several sets of data were collected for this study. First, the sales/income side of the operation was analyzed. The data were collected from cash register receipts for 26 consecutive days of cafeteria operations. This revealed the total sales by income and the number and type of transactions. The data that were collected are found in Table 8.1.

Using this basic data, Zimmerman then constructed a run chart and moving range (MR) chart for transactions. The transactions were shown and the income per day was plotted. The data found in Figure 8.5 showed that Thursdays had the most transactions and Fridays the fewest. All the transactions stayed within the upper and lower control limits of the chart but there were days when the dollar amount of income was lower than the number of transactions, indicating several small sales. To illustrate this, she showed income for each day using a dotted line on the chart. She concluded from this chart that since there was not a close correlation between transactions and income, the number of transactions is not a good predictor of income.

Another control chart plotted the income per day and its moving range. As shown in Figure 8.6, the income stayed within the control limits except on the first two days of school. However, the moving range indicated that the process was not capable of increasing income without making changes. Although the transactions run chart shown in Figure 8.5 indicated the number of customers to be lowest on Fridays, this chart shows that income on Fridays was above average and Monday was generally the lowest dollar sales day.

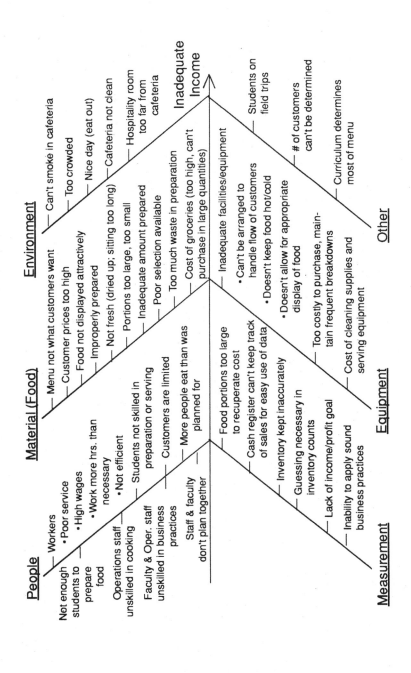

Figure 8.3 – Cause and Effect Diagram Showing Factors Related to Sales Loss at Oshkosh Campus Food Service Program

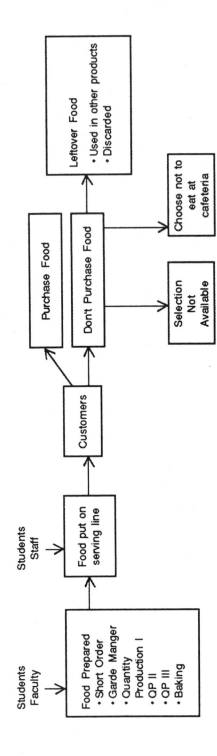

Figure 8.4 – Process Flowchart Showing Food Production and Sales Sequence of the Oshkosh Food Service Operations

Oshkosh Campus Cafeteria

Date	Income	# Transactions
Th9-6	$122.51	133
F 9-7	113.11	124
M 9-10	$166.76	156
T 9-11	189.06	165
W 9-12	177.88	178
Th9-13	208.28	194
F 9-14	196.84	136
M 9-17	$171.13	191
T 9-18	196.47	139
Th9-20	197.20	197
F 9-21	196.27	138
M 9-24	$182.39	171
T 9-25	244.31	231
W 9-26	212.21	219
Th9-27	217.47	239
F 9-28	205.43	139
M 10-1	$194.01	185
T 10-2	204.32	186
W 10-3	199.25	200
Th10-4	222.46	247
F 10-5	192.21	120
M 10-8	$196.64	188
T 10-9	177.23	187
W 10-10	220.87	210
Th10-11	198.97	214
F 10-12	212.29	144
	$5,015.57	4,681
	$\bar{x} = \$192.91$	$\bar{x} = 180$

Table 8.1 – Amount of Income and Number of Transactions Per Day
September 6, 1990 to October 12, 1990

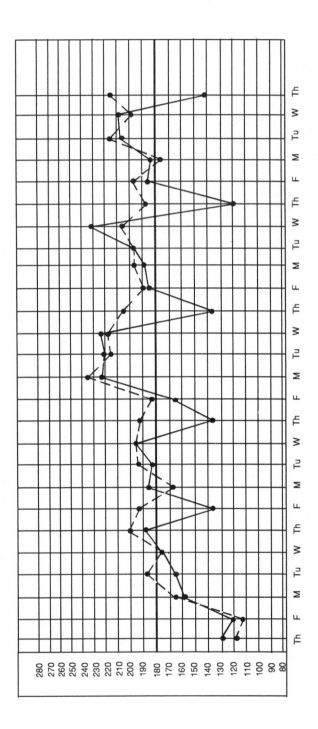

Figure 8.5 – Run Charts Comparing Number of Transactions and Income Per Day

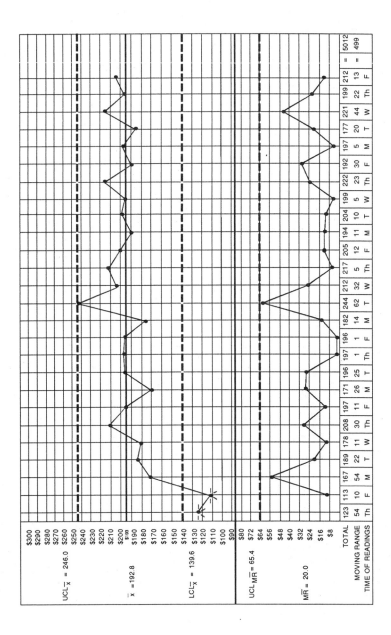

Figure 8.6 – Individual and Moving Range Chart for Income at Oshkosh Campus Cafeteria

   Since these charts did not provide enough information to determine
the causes of income fluctuations, Zimmerman decided to look at
particular types of food sales. She constructed several bar graphs to look
at the relationship between the amounts of income by specific type of
menu item.

   The first bar chart shown in Figure 8.7 shows a comparison of the
percent of transactions with the percent of income for the week October
1–5, 1990. This chart shows that the deli and miscellaneous (salad bar,
sandwiches, fruit, vegetables, desserts) accounted for both the highest
percent of items sold and the income generated. The chart also shows
that beverages and entrees were the higher profit items.

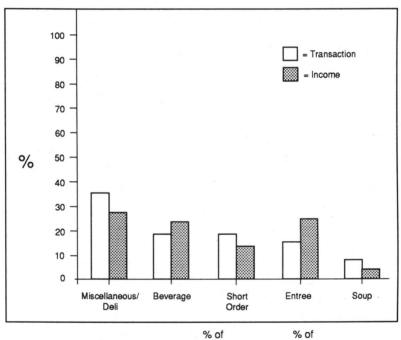

Type	% of Transactions	% of Income
1. Misc/Deli	35.3	27.6
2. Beverage	19.7	24.8
3. Short Order	19.0	15.9
4. Entree	17.1	27.2
5. Soup	9.0	4.5

Figure 8.7 – Bar Chart Showing Type Transaction by Percent Compared
to Percent of Income

This information is also converted to two Pareto charts. The first chart, shown in Figure 8.8, indicates that 74 percent of the sales were miscellaneous/deli, beverages, and short order. The second chart, shown in Figure 8.9, indicates that a different mix and order of miscellaneous/deli, entrees, and beverages accounted for 79.6 percent of income. These two charts lead to additional questions:

- What is wrong with profitability of short order and soup?

- Does the deli hold the key to meeting the goal of making a profit?

	#	%	% accum.
1. Misc/Deli	$331.00	35.3	35.3
2. Beverage	185.00	19.7	55.0
3. Short Order	178.00	19.0	74.0
4. Entree	160.00	17.0	91.0
5. Soup	84.00	9.0	100.0

Total $938.00

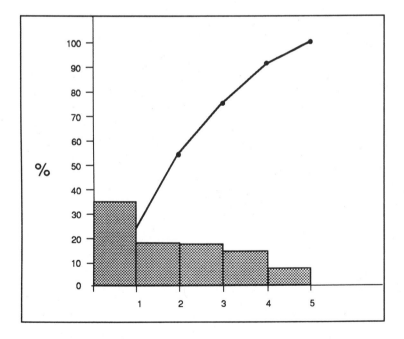

Figure 8.8 – Pareto Chart Showing the Type of Transaction by Percent

	#	%	% accum.
1. Misc/Deli	$278.90	27.6	27.6
2. Entree	275.57	27.2	54.8
3. Beverage	251.05	24.8	79.6
4. Short Order	160.68	15.9	95.5
5. Soup	46.05	4.5	100.0

Total $1,012.25

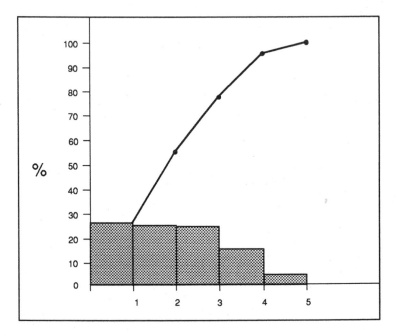

Figure 8.9 – Pareto Chart Showing the Amount and Percent of Income

While there are limitations to this study because only 26 days were used to collect data, this orderly use of food service transactions and income at the Oshkosh campus shows that scientific methods and effective data collection and analysis can be used to both improve processes and assist in making appropriate decisions. The information gathered raised several additional questions, including:

1. Why is Thursday such a popular day at the cafeteria and Monday not?

2. Why is income above average on Fridays when the number of transactions is the lowest of all days?

3. What is the correlation between the number of students in the building and cafeteria utilization?

4. Should the price structure for short order and beverages be changed?

5. How can the sales of higher profit items be increased?

6. What are the "moments of truth" in customer service?

7. What does the customer really want from this service?

However, the information already gathered provided enough data to make some preliminary improvements in the processes that were a part of the food service operations. Using information such as this was certainly better than using hunches or intuition to decide what to do to improve the operation. The faculty, staff, and students who were involved in this project have also developed a greater understanding of the problems and issues. Since they helped gather the data and have seen its application using the scientific tools that were reported in this study, they are more willing to support preliminary changes and future decisions that may be made about the food service operation in Oshkosh. The data collected, together with its analysis, will be an important part of the total data and other factors that will assist the board in making its final decision about food service instruction and operations in Oshkosh.

MEASUREMENT PROJECT: Determining the Economic Feasibility of Offering Programs in the Technical Division on a Year-Round Basis

For several years, the FVTC Technical Division has offered 14 of its 23 programs on a year-round basis. This necessitates offering summer school sections and extending contracts for several faculty and support staff. Recent circumstances have led to questioning the economic feasibility of continuing to schedule these instructional programs on a year-round basis. The two major indicators have been a decline in full-time equivalent students from 115 to 105 during the past three summers and a program student/station utilization decline to less than 50 percent of capacity during the summer of 1990.

Since the college is reaching its property tax levy limit, new finances must be obtained to not only continue regular operations but also to start new costly technical programs for the aviation industry.

Using scientific methods through problem solving and analysis, Dean Virgil Noordyk and his staff undertook a statistical measurement project which will serve as a guide for decision making regarding year-round operation of specific instructional programs in the Technical Division.

The decline of summer enrollments and its causes have been a major point of discussion with the faculty and staff of the division. During a brainstorming session, the staff identified the key causes and effects and these are shown in the cause and effect diagram shown in Figure 8.10.

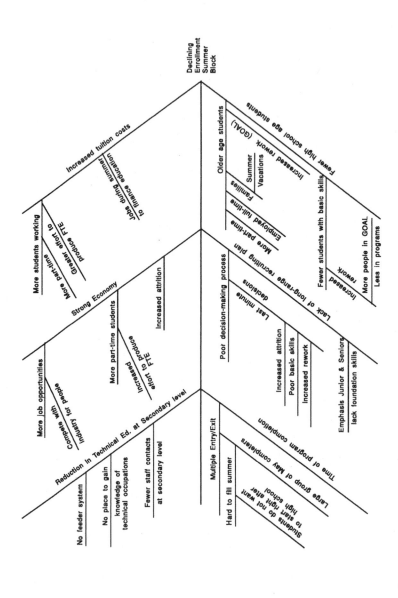

Figure 8.10 – Cause and Effect Diagram Showing Reasons of Declining Enrollments and Effects of Decline

Next, Noordyk gathered information for each of the 14 programs about several items that were then outlined on a summary sheet.

- School FTEs

- Costs for faculty and support staff for summer block

- Revenues from 1990 summer block

- Cost impact if program is discontinued

Using this information he then constructed run charts for each program that showed the costs and revenues. From this information a bar chart was constructed, shown in Figure 8.11, and it already shows the cost/revenue impacts for each program if discontinued. This information assisted Noordyk and his staff in deciding which programs to curtail during the summer block in 1991.

These two examples of process management application illustrate the significance of using data analysis to assist in decision making. With this type of information, the decisions are based on actual data rather than on mere speculation. When this type of scientific method is used by every manager for all major decisions at the college, there will be a significant payback for the costs expended when implementing the quality improvement process. Furthermore, the internal (faculty and staff) and external (students) customers will be more willing to accept these decisions because they know that they have been made with their input, using credible techniques that are supported by good data.

Costing Systems

FVTC has designed an institutional costing system specific to education. The model shows cost projections involved when implementing the quality improvement process. These initial costs become increasingly more credible as cost center data are calculated in the various departments of the school and displayed in a central costing program.

According to ASQC, the costs related to quality include expenditures associated with the prevention of nonconformances and the appraisal of products or services for conformance to stated requirements (or failure to meet requirements).[42]

Calculating and continually monitoring the cost of attaining quality are essential to the process—providing a critical measure of its success. The FVTC Cost Committee followed ASQC guidelines and selected two types of costing elements—the cost of conformance elements and the cost of nonconformance elements. The model contains a listing of these elements together with the criteria used to determine costs under each.

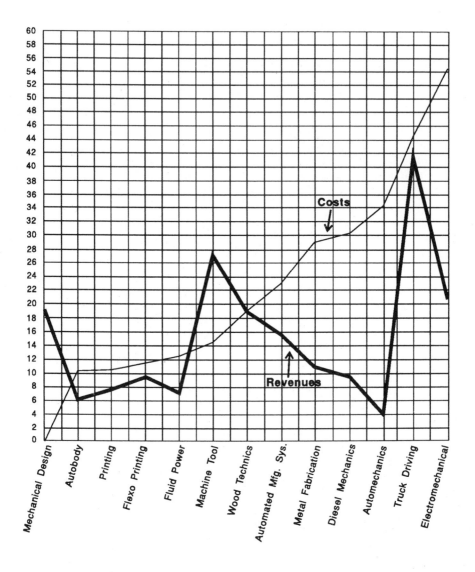

Figure 8.11 – Run Chart Showing Costs and Revenues for
Summer Technical Programs

The costs associated with implementing quality improvement include expenses necessary to make or do things right (cost of conformance) and the costs of doing things wrong (cost of nonconformance).

Costs Of Conformance

Conformance costs are those expenses related to identifying and preventing errors and the process revisions needed to keep the same errors from recurring. Elements included in the FVTC costing model are as follows:

Marketing Research

These are the costs involved in gathering and evaluating data on customers' needs and perceptions about their satisfaction with the school. The amount allocated for this at FVTC model is 50 percent of the research department budget, since the staff spends 50 percent of its time surveying and evaluating data related to the quality process.

Quality Training

The costs for developing and conducting formal training programs to orient employees to quality processes and error prevention are included here. FVTC uses many different levels of training and includes all costs associated with that training.

Quality Coordination

The actual costs required for coordinating the quality improvement process include the salary of the quality coordinator, the supplies and materials used, and other budgeted items for implementing quality improvement.

Quality Monitoring and Auditing

While quality improvement focuses on prevention rather than inspection, an auditing system is still necessary to monitor its level of success. Included are the costs for internal financial control systems used in the process. One-half of the research department's budget is allocated for this..

Wellness Programs

Wellness programs have been established at FVTC to encourage the staff to develop good habits related to diet and fitness. The program result in improved employee productivity and reduced absenteeism. The criterion used to determine these costs is the actual expense for operating wellness programs.

The costs of conformance calculated for FVTC during the 1990-91 fiscal year are shown in Appendix M. Many of these costs were part of the regular school budget prior to the initiation of the quality first process. In those cases, staff time and services were transferred from other cost functions in the budget to the quality process cost allocations.

Costs Of Nonconformance

It is necessary to determine, as closely as possible, the actual expenses involved when the systems within the school are not operating at peak efficiency. While it may be impossible to reach 100 percent efficiency with error-free productivity in all aspects of the school's operation, an attempt should be made to calculate the costs that are associated with deviation from perfection. This creates a staff awareness of the costs associated with poor quality and gives school officials a yardstick to determine improvement. Costs of nonconformance calculated for FVTC using data from the 1989-90 fiscal year are shown in Appendix N. The items included are as follows:

Resource Utilization/Enrollments

There is a cost when maximum enrollment is not maintained in each instructional program. Excess student station costs are determined by analyzing utilization reports that show the ratio of student occupancy to maximum utilization potential. As the department increases the student station utilization, these costs decrease and more money is available for other things.

Rework in Service Departments

These costs are based on estimates of rework that are required because of incorrect, incomplete, or defective products or services. Quality experts estimate that rework accounts for between 20 and 40 percent of service department budgets. The cost allocation used in the FVTC model is 20 percent of each service department's budget. These costs should be looked at as estimates and efforts should be made to refine them as much as possible.

Retention of Students

In addition to the student station utilization costs, there are costs associated with student withdrawals due to loss of state aids and tuition. It has been calculated that for 1990-91, the annual cost at FVTC is approximately $1,900 for each student withdrawal.

Employee Attendance

Costs occur when employees are absent. Included are salaries for overtime and substitutes. The FVTC cost allocation for this is based on the loss of time that is above the national average for employee absence—1.8 percent of total time available to work under regular schedules.

Scheduling of Human Resources

Poor planning and inappropriate management results in inefficient scheduling of teachers, school managers, and technical/clerical staff. Because of this inefficiency, teachers have unequal teaching loads and people are often reassigned to projects that come up at the last minute. Nonconformance and excess costs result. The cost allocation initially estimated for this at FVTC was five percent of the total labor costs for all management and support staff employees. This figure is based on a conservative estimate, since there are substantial costs involved. The cost allocation for unequal teaching schedules varies based on the criterion workload established for each instructional cost center.

Customer Service

Customer complaints about poor instruction and service create costs to investigate, respond to, and resolve the complaint. Included are costs associated with local, state, and federal investigations of alleged affirmative action violations, and other complaints by students. The annual costs associated with this are the salary of one full-time employee. This cost was determined by estimating the time involved in handling complaints brought to the attention of central administration.

There are other internal and external measures, and costs will be added to the measurement and costing model as it matures. The model allows for continued input and modification based on the creativity of the faculty and staff. The only requirement is that these basic principles of measuring and costing be used by those involved:

1. Select measures and cost elements only after determining how each will effectively contribute to the overall purposes and goals of the school.

2. Only collect data if they're going to be used in improving processes.

3. Use available information wherever possible; however, continue to select new measures. Extreme care should be taken to ensure that good data are always used.

4. Always adjust costs for inflation when reporting and using measurement and costs for comparison purposes. Costs don't necessarily have to decrease for productivity to increase.

5. Use caution in announcing measurement and costing results. The overzealous manager can create serious problems by publicizing results out of context.

6. Choose processes to improve that are not undergoing major changes.

As this system of measurement and costing matures, the accuracy of the data and the validity of cost determinations will improve. Cost reductions will continue to become more apparent as this all moves along. However, there are important cost savings that can never be fully determined. There are savings due to new business which comes from improved customer services. There are savings because teachers and other staff are more satisfied with the environment in which they work. There are savings because of new applications by school managers and because of creative projects that are increased by quality-based practices in schools. These savings will all help educators meet new challenges caused by limited financial resources available to schools. Quality concepts, coupled with proper planning and institutional and individual goal setting, are the ingredients to make this occur.

Some Reflections And Thoughts On Application

One of the most difficult tasks in implementing the quality process at FVTC was to encourage faculty and staff to get involved in formal problem-solving and measurement activities. For some reason, they hesitated to use these techniques that are common to most quality movements.

Maybe it was because we didn't provide adequate training in using tools and techniques of problem solving and measurement. We offered one course in understanding the powerful tools of statistical thinking and methods, but the 26 people who took the course didn't apply the processes to any great extent. Perhaps we should have required all managers to take process management courses early in the quality movement, since they were charged with leading the way and encouraging others in their work units.

Several staff, especially in service departments, began to construct graphs and charts to help them identify problems and errors. Most were bar charts or data sheets of various kinds. Occasionally, a Pareto chart or control chart appeared, but they were rare at the start.

One of the best things we did was to define our school's quality elements. These elements, together with conforming requirements and measurement strategies, laid the foundation for constant self-evaluation and analysis. If I were to do it over, I'd define the elements more quickly and convert all evaluation systems accordingly. I'm comfortable now that we've got the elements in place and they're being used in program auditing. However, I'd like to see an even greater use of the elements, especially in work unit self-evaluation.

We hope to rectify our shortcomings in process management and statistical approaches during the next several months. To begin with, we have designed and implemented a process management course with mandatory training in problem-solving and measurement techniques for all school managers. I hope that instructional departments will take the cue and define conforming requirements related to their own processes. The next step will be to identify processes that are creating problems and use scientific approaches to correct them.

We also didn't do very much with calculating costs associated with quality. A basic costing model was set up and some initial costs were estimated, but the projections were weak. As our computer systems get more sophisticated, we'll be able to do a better job of determining costs of conformance and costs of nonconformance. It's encouraging to see actual costs determined for nonconformances such as student withdrawals, poor scheduling, and student station utilization. I'd also like to see our service departments determine the costs associated with doing things over.

When all is said and done, though, I'm satisfied that we did the right thing to move slowly into formal measurement and costing processes. Our initial focus of improving our organizational climate has prepared us to use those tools and techniques common in quality improvement systems in industry.

At the beginning of this chapter, four questions are asked concerning the measuring and costing of quality in education. The FVTC staff, after almost six years of implementing the quality/productivity process, are convinced that the answer to those questions is a resounding "yes."

- Yes, it is possible to describe, judge, and improve the effectiveness of schools;

- Yes, we can correctly and concisely measure and control the variances found in processes common to education;

- Yes, quality in education can be looked at in financial terms as it is in business and industry; and,

- Yes, process management approaches are useful for measurement and analysis in education.

Summary

This chapter describes efforts made at FVTC to incorporate problem-solving and statistical thinking approaches into the quality improvement process. It uses a model developed at the college to integrate measurement, costing, and goal setting in the quest for improvement in education.

Quality elements which are the basis for the model are described in some detail. The use of conforming requirements is advocated with the realization that they are based on customer expectations, are under constant review, and are advanced as ideal criteria which can be met or exceeded.

The college research and evaluation plan focuses on global indicators of success. The plan's integration with other evaluations such as instructional audits and accreditation reviews is expected. With this approach, the college is in a state of constant self-evaluation using its elements as the basis for the continuous review.

A major part of this chapter relates to problem-solving and charting activities in the college. Several examples are shown and described. It's apparent that more sophisticated types of statistical analysis will help improve processes. We have begun to shift toward more objective ways to solve problems and make decisions. Scientific methods and statistical tools are useful in this management shift.

Ways to determine costs related to quality are also described in this chapter. Two types of costs are defined, those related to initiating and continuing quality improvement efforts (costs of conformance) and those related to poor quality practices (costs of nonconformance). Several examples of each are given.

There are several things in education that can be counted, charted, analyzed, and costed with some degree of accuracy. The target is to institute statistical thinking approaches across the organization so that decisions are made based on valid data, obtained from measuring variability differences which are the result of special causes.

While the implementation of the quality process may not necessarily lead to direct and immediate cost reduction for the school, the effort will lead to greater customer satisfaction, better staff relations, and other tangible benefits for the organization. The process itself will create productivity increases that will ultimately lead to greater accountability in the school.

Chapter 9

Using The Quality Process To Evaluate Schools

In spite of reports from national commissions and numerous proposed reforms for education, the major question remains: "How well are our schools preparing students?" Various evaluation systems, including standardized achievement tests and teacher testing programs, have been used in an attempt to answer that question. None appear to have been useful or objective in assessing the job schools are doing. As a result, schools continue to be compared using evaluation systems that create controversy and each new version seeks to be more effective. Typically, standardized test scores are used to compare schools in different communities, states, or from across the country. More recently, American schools are being compared with those from foreign countries.

Most people believe that standardized tests are the best way to measure what students have learned. They contend that the results compared among schools and regions can be used to answer these questions:

- What are our students learning and how do they rank with others at the same grade level?

- How well do our teachers instruct and what are the variables that make differences?

- What is the quality of our schools?

Because of general acceptance, standardized test performance has been the primary criterion used to assess school effectiveness. These tests are usually viewed by the public as being credible and objective. In reality, they have several major limitations.

To begin with, most standardized tests were designed to be convenient to administer and score rather than to measure the logical thinking and reasoning processes used by students. Also, since these tests are used and interpreted across large regions of the country, the outcomes don't take into account the individual thrusts and goals of particular districts or schools. In addition, students who don't plan to go to college don't usually take the tests and therefore the results don't reflect overall school effectiveness. Another weakness is that the tests are usually in multiple-choice format, seeking rapid-fire responses rather than thoughtful answers.

The ways the tests are interpreted may also create problems. Usually the results are compared with other student groups through calculated averages. Most often comparisons are made from among the performances of students from schools of similar size and from similar types of communities (urban, rural, suburban). State-by-state comparisons have also been used with the results reported by different regions of the country.

When one looks at these comparisons and considers both the problems cited above and the socioeconomic diversity of students, it is clear that achievement testing of this sort is not a good indicator of educational quality. While some sort of standardized testing program may be needed, test results should be considered only as one part of a more comprehensive evaluation system used to determine school quality.

Above all, the results of standardized tests should never be used to determine teacher effectiveness. Students enter schools with different competencies, family backgrounds, and experiences, and their test scores could easily misrepresent the effort and quality of the instructor. Therefore, some other type of teacher effectiveness system needs to be developed.

These problems do not mean that standardized achievement tests should be discarded and efforts to determine teacher effectiveness abandoned. It merely requires policymakers and others to use great caution when using and interpreting tests. It also calls for new efforts by testing experts to continually improve their instruments and search for other measures of educational effectiveness.

The quality improvement process suggests customer-driven criteria in addition to standardized testing to determine the overall effectiveness of schools. These criteria are different from traditional testing programs because they focus on processes instead of people. These new approaches require the design of systems that promote quality/productivity techniques proven to work in business and industry. Such systems provide more valid approaches to determine and measure school effectiveness. Outcomes such as test results are used only as an add-on to "process" improvement and they are not used without comparing them also to the goals they were designed to achieve.

The quality process with its focus on accountability requires an orderly study of productivity as a means to determine whether various activities and processes are consistent with the goals and objectives of the organization. This type of system, together with an analysis of the costs associated with each process, will lead to a more effective way to determine whether schools are doing the job they were commissioned to do. Proper application of these techniques will also lead to more effective management, greater harmony in schools, and better results in traditional systems of evaluation.

This chapter describes the evaluation system used at FVTC to determine whether the quality process initiated in 1985 has, indeed, improved the educational programs and services of the college. It will reemphasize some of the techniques and processes which were explained in Chapter 8 on statistical measurement and analysis. This system is based on several assumptions, including:

1. Quality and productivity methods are as useful in improving an organization engaged in service (such as education) as they are in improving a company that produces a product.

2. School personnel, with help from parents and others in the community, can identify their "quality elements" and establish conforming requirements that will become the standards for measurement and statistical analysis.

3. Emphasis in this system will not be placed on people (teachers/staff) and outputs (test scores, dropouts) but rather on the improvement of processes in both instruction and service. With such a focus, the hypothesis is that process improvement will also lead to better teaching and service and greater student achievement.

4. School administrators, through the use of effective leadership skills, can assist teachers and support staff in creating a problem-solving environment that fosters continual improvement.

5. Management and technical processes and transactions in schools must be subjected to continual review. The registration process, course fees, memos, reports, bills, course lists, transcripts, teacher evaluation systems, report cards, and direct contacts with students, parents, and employers need scrutiny.

6. Correct measurement techniques and scientific analysis are paramount whether they are assessing outcomes, as in student achievement; or inputs, such as teacher competence and knowledge; or processes, like student course work, laboratory experiences, or classroom activities.

7. Assessment must be ongoing and structured in a systematic way to promote valid comparisons and determine whether there has been improvement.

8. The organizational climate of the school is used as a barometer of both student and employee satisfaction and management effectiveness. As the organizational climate improves, the teaching/learning process will likewise improve, together with supporting school services.

9. Student satisfaction surveys may be used as single indicators of service effectiveness. As student satisfaction improves, the processes associated with effective learning and teaching will also improve and there will be better outcomes.

10. School costs will decrease automatically if there are fewer mistakes, less rework, fewer delays and snags, continuous review of processes, and better customer service.

Will this system actually improve schools? I believe that it will. Improvement will occur when school managers, faculty, and support staff work together with parents and others in the community to identify requirements based on customer expectations. These requirements, which are defined locally for each school, become the basis for the operation and management of the school. Using defined indicators of success, processes can then be measured and improvement carefully monitored using statistical approaches. All self-analyses, reviews, audits, evaluations, and other forms of assessment are incorporated into the system. The customer-driven criteria are used in regular school decision making and this affects students, faculty, staff, and the overall community. This perpetual application of the quality improvement process leads to organizational changes and better management which focus on team involvement, and a constant review of each and every school transaction. This school effectiveness system creates a better organizational climate which impacts favorably on students, faculty and staff, and all others associated with the school.

The outcomes, such as student achievement and school/community relationships, will also improve. The use of proven business methods is bound to create schools that feature internal staff and the community working together toward educational excellence.

Barometers Of Success At Fox Valley Technical College

FVTC staff believe that the college will automatically improve if the quality process is properly applied. They have identified criteria which, when met or exceeded, become determinants of the school's success. Measurement and analysis of those criteria become the barometers that show that the process is producing results.

As stated several times before, the criteria for determining success at the college are quality elements that the staff have written along with conforming requirements. Measurement strategies have also been identified and a systematic research design is in place to ensure that there is constant review. The standards are continually readjusted as customer expectations change. The ultimate goal is to exceed customer expectations.

The comprehensive research system includes the use of several surveys listed below that are conducted on a regular basis.

- **Organizational Climate Survey**—measures staff perceptions of supervisors, peers, and the organization as a whole.

- **Student Satisfaction Survey**—assesses student satisfaction with instruction and key student services.

- **Employer Satisfaction Survey**—determines satisfaction of employers who have hired graduates of the college.

- **Community Perception Survey**—measures the public image of FVTC.

- **Graduate Placement Survey**—identifies placement statistics, graduates' employers, and starting salaries six months after graduation.

- **Five-Year Graduate Survey**—tracks progress of graduates after five years.

- **Regional Studies**—identifies the educational needs of employers, residents, and high school students in the outlying regions of the district.

The results of these surveys are analyzed by the school's research staff and written reports are prepared and distributed to the internal staff and the public. The TQLC and the quality committees recommend action plans for areas identified through the surveys needing improvement.

In addition to these surveys, instructional and service department audits are conducted by external teams to determine if their services are meeting or exceeding defined expectations. Special surveys are also conducted when needed by the individual departments, committees, or other groups. Ongoing problem-solving activities occurring in the work units and district-wide studies conducted by teams create an atmosphere of a continued quest for improvement.

As described in Chapter 8, problem-solving activities focus on unique problems identified by faculty and staff. Using scientific methods and statistical tools, staff determine root causes of problems and take action to eliminate them forever. Charting and statistical analysis are used to measure process variability and monitor improvement. The goal is to eliminate special causes that show up outside the calculated control limits and focus on both maintaining and improving stable processes through ongoing reduction of common cause variation.

School-Wide Quality Audits

While surveys, statistical analysis, and cost benefit reviews are used to monitor the quality process, external quality audits are conducted to ensure that outside perspectives are applied. These outside reviews occur regularly under the direction of the TQLC. People external to the school with experience in quality improvement processes are selected as the audit team. The quality coordinator is placed in charge of the evaluation.

The first quality audit was conducted at FVTC in 1990. An ad hoc staff committee was appointed to select the outside audit team and established the audit guidelines. The committee members played important roles in assisting the audit team members during the two-day review which included an evaluation of both written materials and interviews with students and staff.

A summary of the 1990 external audit report is found in Appendix O. The audit team made several recommendations and these were converted to action plans by the Total Quality Leadership Council.

Malcolm Baldrige Examination

While the external audit was useful, some problems were identified by the internal audit committee and the TQLC. Most of the problems were related to the logistics of the auditing process and the criteria that were used. Shortly after the audit was completed, the decision was made to review the Malcolm Baldrige National Quality Award Examination as the possible criteria for future quality audits.

The Malcolm Baldrige National Quality Award is an annual award to recognize U.S. companies that excel in quality achievement and quality management. The award promotes the following:

- Awareness of quality

- Understanding of the requirements for quality

- Sharing of information on successful strategies and the benefits derived during implementation

Companies who wish to participate in the award process submit applications and complete the award examination based on quality excellence criteria. When applicants respond to the criteria, they provide information and data that are used as a basis for selecting award-winning companies. The application examination is also used to diagnose overall quality management.[43]

The examination guidelines were established for use by "for profit" businesses and subsidiaries, and schools are not currently eligible for Malcolm Baldrige awards. The examination is useful, however, in nonprofit organizations and public schools. The criteria help to summarize strengths, determine areas for improvement, and identify quality management profiles. They incorporate a rigorous and objective evaluation of a school's total quality system, including underlying services and customer satisfaction. In the actual Malcolm Baldrige selection process, on-site reviews are conducted by several experts. At FVTC, this review will be conducted by external quality specialists selected by the TQLC.

The examination is divided into seven categories that cover the major components of a total quality management system. Each category is divided into examination items which identify the key elements within each category. The examination also contains a section titled "Areas to Address" for each item. The examination categories and the maximum points available for each are summarized in Appendix P. Together, the seven examination categories address all major components of an integrated, prevention-based quality system built around continuous quality improvement.[44]

To show an example of how the Malcolm Baldrige criteria could be used in education and to provide a summary of the FVTC quality process strengths and weaknesses, a self-analysis of the overall quality management and environment at FVTC is given using those criteria. This summary is shown below.

Leadership

This category measures the extent of leadership by the chief executive officer and the senior executives of the organization. It examines commitment made to the quality process and actions taken to enhance the movement. Also examined are the organization's quality leadership in the external community and how it integrates its public responsibilities with its quality values and practices.

FVTC Self Analysis

The college board, director/president, and vice presidents provide the overall leadership for the process. The director/president has a set of quality-related goals that are agreed to and evaluated by the school board. The goals are based on input from the administrative team and the QIC. Vice presidents and other senior managers have at least one annual goal on quality.

All senior executives are heavily involved in quality and are active in learning more about quality by attending workshops and seminars and reviewing literature on quality. During 1990, the director/president and a faculty member gave a presentation at the Annual ASQC Congress in San Francisco. He accompanied two faculty members on a visit to Australia where the team conducted several workshops for educators from throughout the country. He also taught a graduate course in school administration that included several units on quality and productivity in educational administration.

The external audit team recommended that senior executives provide even greater leadership to the quality movement. The audit team called for more active, verbal communications and fewer written documents. As a result of this suggestion, an action plan was prepared that outlines activities for 1990-91 for each of the senior executives.

Every day they are on campus, the executive team spends time with both internal and external customers. They try to demonstrate quality values in everyday administration. They have established a major goal to integrate quality more directly into everyday operations.

Poor communication was also identified as a weakness. Data from the annual Organizational Climate Survey, shown in Table 9.1, indicate that the flow of communication in the school is low, with the school-wide average being 2.66 on a 5-point scale. The data show that improvement is needed at all levels of the school. Senior executives have been targeted by the analysis to be more accessible to staff and to communicate more effectively how decisions about various things will affect the various departments of the school.

In an effort to improve communications, the administration decided on two new approaches:

1. Employment of an outside consultant team to assess communications in the organization and recommend a plan for continuous improvement

2. Conduct of two conflict resolution workshops involving all levels of personnel and board members with a focus on improving communications. Approximately 50 people have participated.

To demonstrate commitment, the board adopted a policy on quality and the District's Strategic Directions show quality improvement as a major thrust of the college. Two other board policies related to customer satisfaction have been adopted.

ORGANIZATIONAL CLIMATE	1990	1989
Communication Flow	2.66	2.63
Decision-Making Practices	2.60	2.58
Concern for People	2.96	2.79
Influence and Control	3.13	3.01
Job Challenge	3.98	3.89
Job Reward	2.46	2.35
Job Clarity	3.23	3.16
Organization of Work	2.90	2.88
Absence of Bureaucracy	2.81	2.69
Coordination	2.89	2.89
Work Interdependence	3.51	3.42

1=Very Dissatisfied   2=Somewhat Dissatisfied   3=Neither Satisfied Nor Dissatisfied
4=Somewhat Satisfied   5=Very Satisfied

Table 9.1 – Organizational Climate Survey—Communications, 1990 vs. 1989

To assist entering students, a comprehensive basic skills program has been initiated. In 1990-91, over 6,000 students took at least one basic skills course. The college is also offering "College Survival Skills" courses to help students adjust to the college environment. Special programs for displaced workers and "at-risk" students have been initiated; and specialists and counselors are available to assist handicapped, disadvantaged, and other students with special needs.

Another identified weakness is the lack of school-wide strategy for involving all levels of management in the quality movement. To correct this, a management task force was appointed to define the roles and functions of managers and to design a special training program for them. A 36-hour process management course was offered in 1990-91 with all administrators and managers participating.

In another effort to encourage commitment, each manager was asked to prepare a written report of his or her work unit's involvement in quality and meet with the director/president to discuss individual progress in that effort. A percentage of the salary increase for management was allocated for efforts in quality.

Table 9.2 shows results of the Organizational Climate Survey which indicate that "peer relationships" at the college are quite good. The Computer Integrated Manufacturing (CIM) Network is an excellent example of cooperation between different personnel levels and departments. Several faculty and staff from 13 different departments developed this network and, as a result, the college has been named a national training center in CIM for IBM. One tangible result of that affiliation with IBM was the donation of equipment and software which was valued in excess of $1 million.

PEER RELATIONSHIPS	1990	1989
Peer Support	3.82	3.81
Peer Team Building	3.43	3.44
Peer Goal Emphasis	3.66	3.62
Peer Work Facilitation	3.38	3.32

1=Very Dissatisfied   2=Somewhat Dissatisfied   3=Neither Satisfied Nor Dissatisfied
4=Somewhat Satisfied   5=Very Satisfied

Table 9.2 – Organizational Climate Survey—Peer Relationships,
1990 vs. 1989

A major goal of the college is to integrate the quality process into everyday management and operations. There are several areas where duplication exists between the structure for quality and ongoing operations. The potential of conflicting roles between the administrative council and the QIC has been identified as one such integration problem. It is anticipated that the two councils will merge soon.

Another Malcolm Baldrige examination criterion on leadership relates to promoting quality awareness in the community. There have been several major initiatives at FVTC. The Quality Academy has been organized to assist other schools who wish to pursue the quality improvement movement. A regional Quality Network provides monthly programs about quality for people from district business and industry. A Quality/Productivity Resource Center (Q/PRC) provides quality-related media and other resources for the community. These external activities have resulted in phenomenal growth in enrollment in courses and workshops related to quality. Another outcome has been the design and implementation of a two-year associate degree program to prepare quality/productivity specialists.

Information And Analysis

This category examines the scope, validity, and use of data and information that underlie the college's total quality management system. It looks at how the college "manages by fact." Information used for planning and budgeting is also examined.

FVTC uses the quality elements as a major criteria for determining what to include in the quality-related data/information system. The college has good baseline data but needs more specific measurement goals and a plan for linking data bases. For each conforming requirement, measurement strategies have been identified. A research/evaluation system has been established and timetables have been set for conducting surveys and gathering school-wide data. This system provides a comprehensive approach to determining the extent of improvement in the organization.

Internal data are prepared and distributed to staff in a systematic way. Most of the data compare various cost centers and programs with each other over the past three years. There is an annual "mini-audit" which provides a computer report that analyzes several criteria for each instructional program. The report earmarks certain programs for comprehensive instructional audit by an external team because of identified weaknesses.

In addition to the annual mini-audit for programs, a comprehensive audit of five to seven programs is conducted each year. A separate team of outside experts spends two days reviewing each program and prepares a written report for the administration and the Curriculum Committee of the board. The quality elements serve as the criteria for the audit.

A monthly report titled "Indicators of District Health" is distributed to the board and staff. The report shows trends in the various instructional divisions of the college through graphic and numeric information that includes three-year comparative data on full-time equivalent students, unduplicated head counts, student withdrawals, graduates, and student applications.

Two other major studies were conducted in 1990. A team of internal staff and outside consultants examined future computer software and hardware needs. All faculty and staff were invited to complete a written survey on their computer needs, and over 100 personal interviews of staff were conducted. Using this information, a long-range informational system plan was prepared. As a result, a five-year timetable and budget was adopted by the board and implementation of the $2.5 million plan started in 1990. This new equipment and software will enhance the quality-related information system.

One weakness that has been identified in this section is that the college has not collected or used benchmark data in a formal way. While several staff members went on group benchmarking visits to innovative community/technical colleges in Florida, Minnesota, Illinois, and Ohio in 1989-90, the data and information were collected and analyzed in a haphazard way. The college plans to establish a more formal plan to identify benchmark schools and businesses and gather data systematically.

Strategic Quality Planning Process

This category demonstrates how the college has integrated quality improvement planning into overall business planning. It examines how the school's short-term and long-term priorities are set to achieve and/or sustain a quality leadership position among other two-year colleges.

The college is divided into instructional and service work units based on functions. Sometimes referred to as a department, each work unit is an accounting cost center. Operational plans and budgets are developed by the faculty and staff of each work unit in an attempt to integrate the operational plan with the required resources.

The mission, purposes, and strategic directions of the college are approved by the board, following input from college personnel and people in the community. Each instructional program has an advisory committee that meets at least twice a year. Minutes of the meetings are circulated to staff and board members. Several other district-wide committees are established.

One example is an 18-member Chief Executive Officer Council that meets three times each year. The CEO Council meets with the college director/president and provides business/industry advice to the college. For example, the idea to begin quality/productivity training programs originated from the council. During 1991–92 a small business CEO Council will be organized to focus on the needs of small firms. Additionally, the director/president has several presidents' luncheons during the year to encourage information sharing between the college and the CEOs who attend. Over 100 senior executives attended these luncheons during 1990–91.

An annual list of Operational Thrusts is prepared by the administrative council, reviewed by the TQLC and union officials, and approved by the board. Appendix Q shows the Operational Thrusts for 1990-91. The director/president's objectives are linked to the thrusts and are evaluated during an annual board retreat. Each administrative unit also prepares annual goals and objectives that have been integrated with the work unit operational plans.

A long-range cost containment plan was prepared in 1990, reviewed by several teams, and adopted by the board. It contains projections and priorities for programs, services, personnel, and capital projects. A capital financial plan is included and productivity targets are listed. Major priorities related to quality improvement were identified as follows:

- Increased staff training and education and the design of individual professional development plans

- Greater involvement by senior executives and middle managers in the quality process

- Further integration of the quality process with everyday operations and services

- Increased problem-solving activities and the use of the scientific methods and statistical tools in decision making

While the strategic planning process needs some streamlining, there is evidence that it has improved over the past few years. It has been identified as one of the "strength" areas of the college. Faculty and staff involvement has been very good and some excellent planning documents have been prepared. Further integration of operational plans with the budgeting process is encouraged.

Human Resource Utilization

This category examines the effectiveness of the college in developing and realizing the full potential of the faculty and staff. It looks at human resource development at all levels of the school and evaluates whether the environment is conducive to good teaching, quality leadership, and personal and organizational growth.

The Human Resources Administrative Unit of the college has the responsibility to initiate the integration of the quality process with regular school services and operations. Several new initiatives have begun, including an Employee Wellness program, a leadership development thrust, staff recognition events, quality commitment activities, WIM/NIN Bargaining, and an Employee Assistance program.

The Human Resources Unit works with several quality committees. For example, the Education Committee prepares the plan for education and training for the district and implements it in cooperation with the training director and vice president of Human Resources. The Recognition Committee plans the programs to recognize faculty and staff. Committee members are in charge of the annual quality awards. The Customer Service Committee makes recommendations to improve services to both internal and external customers and works with the Human Resources Unit to implement their plan. Committee members are responsible for the college suggestion system.

Demographic data on all full-time personnel are collected and analyzed continually. The district routinely compiles the following information about faculty and staff:

- Age and experience levels
- Salary and classification levels
- Certification attainment information
- Attendance records
- Educational/training data
- Recognition and achievements

One of the quality elements is directly related to human resources. The conforming requirements of this element are analyzed as a part of each instructional and service audit. Data obtained through the annual Organizational Climate Survey pinpoint educational/training needs. A subsequent survey of staff identifies other training needs. The college training director coordinates education and training needs and assists in the design of individual professional development plans.

The Quality Academy is the quality improvement training wing of the school. It works with the college training director to coordinate the design of curriculum and implement training for all employees. The staff education program has been good, but it has not been sufficient. All personnel received initial quality awareness training. Executives, top-level managers, and board members received additional training in quality process application. All new personnel receive quality orientation and awareness training early in their employment.

Phase II training has begun for all full-time personnel. The Phase II training plan, which was approved by the Total Quality Leadership Council, is explained in Chapter 3 and is outlined in Figure 3.2. The Phase II training is specific to the three personnel levels: faculty, support/technical staff, and management/administration. A course designer/trainer has been appointed for each level of training and a staff committee for each group assisted in the design of the courses. The specific topic areas are shown in Figure 9.1.

Group	Training Thrust	Length
Senior Executives Administrative Council All Managers	Process Management Problem-Solving Statistical Thinking Team Building Customer Service	36 hours
Faculty/Counselors	Teaching Techniques Functional Training Problem-Solving Customer Service Team Building	36 hours
Support and Technical Staff	Customer Service Personal Development Skills Team Building Problem Solving	36 hours
Adjunct Faculty	Quality Awareness Teaching Techniques	Various

Figure 9.1 – Phase II Staff Training Plan Topic Areas

There were two major cross functional studies related to human resources during 1989-90. One dealt with management and the other was related to *time*. A management task force was organized to determine the preferred roles and functions of managers and to recommend training and selection criteria for new managers. Members of the task force wrote the quality element on management. A study of the time issue was conducted by the faculty union president and a school manager. Their report has been disseminated to all personnel and their recommendations have been reviewed by a group of management and union personnel and the TQLC. A conflict resolution workshop was facilitated by an outside consultant in an effort to improve communications, break down barriers, and resolve issues which were identified as problems in the study. The *time* issue has not been resolved.

One of the positive outcomes of the quality process has been the gradual improvement of the college's organizational climate. Data to support this are found later in this chapter. Future impacts of the quality improvement process on the structure and organization of the college are targeted as follows:

- Breakdown of hierarchical staff levels and a "flattening" of the organizational structure

- Initiation of differentiated staffing patterns and a shift in roles and functions of personnel

- Greater team involvement, including the establishment of self-directed teams in all departments

- New methods of structuring teaching and assignments to permit greater opportunities for training and professional growth

- New forms of compensation based on roles and functions

Several recognition activities have been developed to help acknowledge contributions of faculty and staff. The following awards are given at various times during the year:

- **Great Performance Awards**—to recognize performances which exceed customer expectations

- **TEMPO Awards**—to recognize time, effort, merit, and performances classified as excellent

- **Cutting Edge Award**—to recognize contributions which provide exemplary leadership and skill to the college and community

- **Quality Award**—to recognize those who have made significant and measurable impact on the college through teamwork and problem solving

More than 50 work unit teams were originally organized in the college. Each selected its team leader and decided on the problems to solve. Some training was conducted on team building but it was not enough. Some of the teams did not function well and a few disbanded. Future training has been directed toward improving skills in team building and problem solving in the college. In addition to the work unit teams, there are currently ten active quality-related college-wide committees. Two district-wide problem-solving teams are active in specific projects.

There have been several human resource problem areas identified through the Organizational Climate Survey and the external quality audit. The major ones deal with communications and staff relations. The college is attempting to address these in a number of ways.

As stated earlier in Chapter 7, the director/president has monthly luncheon meetings with the union officers from the faculty and support staff. The quality coordinator and college vice presidents attend with the director/president. Several issues have been resolved as the result of these meetings.

There has also been a major effort on the part of the senior executives to be more accessible and approachable by faculty and staff. An annual staff appreciation social event is sponsored by the executives, and staff attendance has been excellent. Information and data that, in the past, have been reserved only for top management are now being shared regularly with the union officers. The union officers and administrators agree that the number of grievances has declined sharply. Figure 9.2 supports this contention.

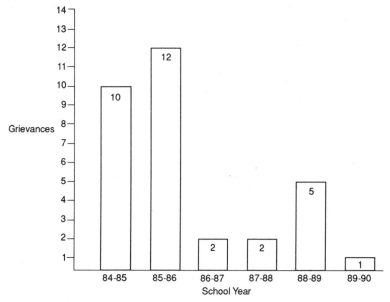

Figure 9.2 – Number of Grievances at FVTC

Other major efforts have been directed toward improving relationships between administration and personnel. Multi-year contracts have been agreed upon with both unions, and the management compensation plan was established for a two-year period. Early retirement options have been arranged based on individuals' requests, and flexible work schedules are used in several departments. The board and the unions have agreed to use "win-win" bargaining concepts during the next round of contract negotiations.

In an attempt to encourage greater communications, all personnel have been given access to an electronic mail system (PROFS) and an electronic bulletin board. Board members also have access to the system through computers in their homes linked to PROFS through phone modem dial-up. This access provides opportunities for all parties to send and receive information.

To improve management and create more autonomy, each division of the school is given the opportunity to reorganize its management structure based on the needs and requirements of the team members. All college administrative units have been encouraged to "flatten" their structures to provide greater access to personnel and provide greater decision-making involvement by all staff.

Innovation and risk taking have been encouraged at the college. Some examples of initiatives which were implemented during 1989-90 include:

- Developed a nationally recognized Computer Integrated Manufacturing (CIM) Network

- Established a guaranteed retraining policy that provides free training and services to graduates who are unable to get employment in their field of study

- Initiated a customer suggestion system that enables students and staff to offer compliments and make suggestions

- Conducted time and management studies to examine staff time requirements and identify preferred management profiles

- Reviewed and modified the computer/technology information system based on broad staff input

- Eliminated smoking in all buildings through the initiation of district-wide policies

- Established a recycling approach for the handling and disposal of waste materials

The Organizational Climate Survey reports yearly changes in employee satisfaction of the work environment. Figure 9.3 shows the results of the Organizational Climate Survey for the past four years. These results indicate that there has been significant improvement in six of eleven items that are related to organizational climate rated by over 85 percent of the employees. Other improvements occurred in supervisory leadership, peer relations, and end results. Areas of decreasing satisfaction have been investigated and action plans for their improvement have been developed.

Staff satisfaction is also determined using certain items on the Organizational Climate Survey. Figure 9.4 outlines the results.

ORGANIZATIONAL CLIMATE	1990	1989	1988	1987	Change 1987 vs. 1990
Communication Flow	2.66	2.63	2.69	2.61	+.05
Decision-making Practices	2.60▲	2.58	2.59	2.47	+.13
Concern for People	2.96▲	2.79	2.84	2.79	+.17
Influence and Control	3.13▲	3.01	2.82	2.83	+.30
Job Challenge	3.98▲	3.89	3.89	3.83	+.15
Job Reward	2.46▲	2.35	2.28	2.31	+.15
Job Clarity	3.23	3.16	3.15	3.14	+.09
Organization of Work	2.90	2.88	2.99	2.94	-.04
Bureaucracy	2.81	2.69	2.57	2.70	+.11
Coordination	2.89	2.89	2.93	2.81	+.08
Work Interdependence	3.51▲	3.42	3.25	3.24	+.27

▲ Areas rated notably higher in 1990 than in 1987

1=Very Dissatisfied	3=Neither Satisfied Nor Dissatisfied	5=Very Satisfied
2=Somewhat Dissatisfied	4=Somewhat Satisfied	

Figure 9.3 – Organizational Climate Ratings by Employees
4-Year Results

END RESULTS	1990	1989
Group Functioning	3.70	3.66
Group Performance	4.03	4.01
Individual Performance	4.25	4.25
Satisfaction	3.51	3.43
Goal Integration	3.27	3.20

1=Very Dissatisfied   2=Somewhat Dissatisfied   3=Neither Satisfied Nor Dissatisfied
4=Somewhat Satisfied   5=Very Satisfied

Figure 9.4 – Organizational Climate Survey—Satisfaction, 1990 vs. 1989

There are several examples of faculty and staff who were retrained because their former jobs were redesigned or eliminated. In 1989-90, a faculty member was retrained and reassigned to a new instructional department because his program was eliminated. Two management staff requested and were granted early retirement privileges with part-time contracts in new positions. In an effort to improve professional development possibilities for staff, the college increased its 1990-91 professional growth budget by $60,000.

The major long-term and short-term human resource priorities that have been established by various committees are as follows:

(Long-Term)

- Integrate the quality process into regular programs, operations, and services.

- Develop an individualized professional and personal development plan for each FVTC faculty and staff member and monitor its implementation.

- Increase the professional growth budget to at least three percent of the total annual budget.

(Short-Term)

- Implement Phase II of quality process training for all personnel.

- Appoint internal consultants to assist staff in team building, process management, and customer service.

- Gain full acceptance and commitment of all senior executives and middle managers to the quality improvement process.

- Institute problem-solving activities in each work unit of the district with continued movement toward the use of scientific methods and the basic statistical tools.

- Merge the Quality Improvement Council and the Administrative Council into one governing body.

Quality Assurance Of Products And Services

This category examines the systematic approaches used by the college for total quality control of goods and services. Evaluated is the integration of quality control through process design and measurement.

In a technical college, customer requirements are determined by those who hire graduates. Therefore, a system of job analysis is needed to match course competencies with job tasks. Mastery of the competencies by students is required, and criterion reference examinations are used to measure whether students have met them. At FVTC, the competencies are validated through a combination of processes, including job surveys, DACUM (Developing A Curriculum) systems, and advisory committee assistance. Validation of the competencies also occurs when analyzing the placement success rates of graduates and when conducting employer satisfaction surveys. Therefore, the competency-based approach used at the college is, in itself, a quality control system.

There are several other control systems at FVTC. Success indicators have been identified for each instructional program, and the placement and successful advancement of graduates in employment are used for this purpose. Control systems have also been established to retain more students in programs and reduce college dropout rates.

One such effort to improve retention was the initiation of a new course, "College Survival Skills." The course was designed by a team of faculty who used student input to develop a curriculum that addressed incoming student needs. Retention rates of 185 students who took the course were compared with a similar number of students with similar characteristics who did not take the course. The results of the study, as noted in Figure 9.5, showed that there was a 16 percent increase in student retention for those who completed the course. Other similar studies are being conducted to determine if this course should be mandatory for all new students.

Another attempt to assist incoming students is the creation of a career-development process at the college. Special groups of students, such as displaced homemakers, older adults, economically disadvantaged people, and displaced workers, are provided with individualized and group instruction to assist them in their occupational and program choices.

In an effort to improve retention rates, faculty have established basic skill attainment prerequisites for their students. All program students are tested using a nationally validated instrument (ASSET) and, based on their scores, are counseled into developmental courses in reading, mathematics, English, writing, science, and social studies. Additionally, a computerized writing laboratory was set up in which students can receive special assistance from faculty in improving writing skills. The writing laboratory is a free service of the college.

Other systems of control include accreditation and licensure requirements. FVTC has been accredited since 1971 and in 1985 received a ten-year reaccreditation by the North Central Association of Universities, Colleges, and Technical Schools. Several college programs have also attained accreditation status by national agencies. Graduates

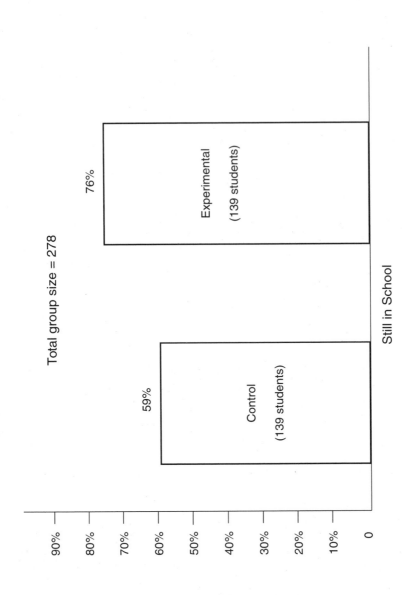

Figure 9.5 – Percent of Students Who Remained in School After Completing the College Survival Course (Experimental) Compared to Other Students (Control) Who Did Not Take the Course

in programs such as Nursing and Occupational Therapy Assistant take licensure exams. The success ratios of nursing graduates on State Board Examinations are benchmarked with other nursing schools.

As mentioned earlier, the "Survey of Organizations," published by Rensis Likert Associates, Inc., and used with permission of the University of Michigan Institute for Social Research, is a control system used to evaluate the college organizational climate. It is a nationally validated survey that contains 128 items organized into 28 "indexes." Some sample questions from the survey are found in Appendix R.

The authors of the "Survey of Organizations" believe that the real causes of problems in organizations like FVTC are found in the climate that includes conditions, policies, and practices of the environment. They believe that organizational climate, leadership, and peer relationships will determine the end results for any institution. The instrument measures those three critical areas.

A major goal of the quality process is the improvement of the work environment and increased personnel satisfaction. By surveying all personnel on a regular basis, the college can note changes through comparative analysis. Survey results reflect changes in climate and may be used as indicators that the quality process is making a difference. As shown earlier in Figure 9.3, several of the indexes had significant improvement over the past four years.

In addition to compiling survey results on a college-wide basis, the results are also compiled by personnel level. Results from the survey are calculated for each manager who supervises at least three employees. The manager is then able to compare his or her results with the average scores of the entire college. The survey becomes a good communications tool when managers share results with their team members and discuss ways to improve. It is further used by the manager as a basis for the establishment of individual improvement goals.

While the research/evaluation system of the college is rather comprehensive, the use of statistical approaches within work units has been identified as a weakness. The use of scientific methods and the application of the statistical tools occurs only on a limited basis in most departments. Collection of data is occurring and several departments are charting data regularly, but analysis of data and determination of variation has been weak. There is increasing evidence, however, that staff are now beginning to use statistical methods to establish control limits, plot variability, and show which items are out of control due to special causes.

A major goal of the college is to foster a "statistical thinking" philosophy. To promote this, all managers received 36 hours of training .in problem solving, team building, and statistical process control during 1990-91. Each will pilot measurement applications in his or her work unit. The school will benchmark the Organizational Climate Survey results by comparing them with other schools using the Rensis Likert data base.

The Continuous Process Improvement (CPI) system has also been identified by staff as a weakness. It has been used in the past five years as a means to identify process upsets. Once problems are identified, the staff, through brainstorming, attempt to determine root causes and then take steps to eliminate the problem forever. However, problems have occurred with this system largely because it is often misunderstood and misused. Modifications in the CPI process and an increase in the proper use of problem-solving techniques and statistical tools are anticipated during 1991.

Another area targeted for improvement relates to a primary supplier to the college. The 27 public school districts with 37 area high schools provide graduates who ultimately enroll at the college. Requirements for these potential students (recommended high school competencies) are being written in several program areas and are being shared with high school faculty. Dual credit programs with high schools and other articulated curriculum projects have been initiated in 23 public school districts. Several 2 + 2, prep-tech programs have been started. Advanced standing and advanced credit is granted to students who come to the college with experiences in occupational education and extensive job experiences.

The quality coordinator annually prepares a report that shows the strengths and weaknesses of the quality process. It is presented to the board and distributed to all faculty and staff. All surveys that are conducted are summarized and analyzed in writing by research department staff, and these reports are shared freely with college personnel, the board, and the community.

Quality Results

This category examines quality levels and improvement based on objective measures which are derived from customer requirements. Also examined are quality levels in relation to competing colleges.

FVTC's primary product is competent graduates for business and industry. In addition, the college provides instruction to those currently employed to keep them upgraded in their jobs. An annual report of these two activities is prepared. In 1989-90, the graduate placement report revealed that 93 percent of the graduates obtained jobs. In addition, the college led the Technical College System in customized and technical assistance contracts with business and industry. Almost one-third of all contracts written in Wisconsin were by FVTC.

Because there is a shortage of students who attend technical colleges in Wisconsin, the college is attempting to recruit greater numbers of high school graduates. Currently, only 12 percent of the current high school graduating students attend classes at technical colleges immediately after high school.

To reverse this trend, FVTC has used several strategies:

- Increase marketing efforts with area high school students and their parents.

- Establish transfer agreements with four-year schools so that students can first attend technical college and later go on to a four-year university to complete the baccalaureate degree.

- Provide career information programs in the junior high schools of the district.

- Encourage business and industry to assist in recruiting student applicants.

- Initiate a guaranteed retraining policy that provides free instruction and service to graduates who do not get a job in their occupational area.

- Expand customized training in order to decrease reliance on four-year graduates.

It is difficult to compare the college's quality process with industry averages because there has not been enough statistical data collected to be used for comparative purposes. However, the college has targeted several schools to compare some of the major initiatives of the school. These include the following:

- Other technical colleges in Wisconsin (placement of graduates and program/service costs)

- Other national CIM training centers for IBM (use of technology)

- Delaware Community College, Pennsylvania (quality process)

- Miami-Dade Community College, Florida (basic skills/entrance testing)

- Houston Community College, Texas (quality process)

- Hawkeye Institute of Technology, Iowa (quality process)

- University of North Carolina (multi-media technology)

The major trends that have been identified and the principal conclusions that have been reached as the result of the quality improvement process can be summarized as follows:

- Organizational climate and student satisfaction can be improved significantly as shown in the data collected over the past four years.

- The quality process model used by the college is appropriate for education even though continued modification is needed.

- The college's credibility with business and industry is enhanced by the quality process, as shown by major increases in the number of customized training and technical assistance contracts.

- Faculty and staff are generally receptive to the concepts and application of quality improvement processes.

- Problem-solving activities can lead to continuous improvement with the proper use of scientific methods and statistical tools.

- Teams can be used effectively in a technical college for problem solving, process improvement, and shared decision making.

- Reducing vertical hierarchial structures and installing more horizontal structures will provide greater communication to staff.

There have been special challenges and problems associated with the initiation of quality improvement processes at FVTC. Most problems are similar to those which have been reported in business and industry when quality concepts are initiated. These challenges and problems have been identified throughout this book. Based on over five years of experience, the following suggestions are offered to educators considering the implementation of quality improvement processes in their schools:

1. Continued attention, commitment, and training is required, as the improvement process is slow and gradual.

2. Extra training and support is required for managers to assist them in coping with problems and challenges as the new systems are initiated.

3. Training in team building, problem solving, and customer service is required for all school personnel.

4. Special efforts are needed to improve communications and keep personnel informed about changes.

5. Comprehensive application of quality principles across the institution is preferred over pilot application in smaller school units.

Customer Satisfaction

This category examines the school's knowledge of the customer, overall customer service systems, responsiveness, and its ability to meet and exceed customer expectations. Current levels and trends in customer satisfaction are also examined.

The college has established market segments through the use of surveys and an external marketing advisory committee. A district marketing plan has been published and is being used. The marketing quality element has conforming requirements and these are used when analyzing enrollment trends.

To improve program quality, the college has a very extensive advisory committee structure. Over 700 advisory members help the college maintain program relevancy and assist in marketing to prospective students.

The close ties with business and industry through customized training and technical assistance programs have also helped to create and maintain program quality and relevancy. This economic development effort has also led to several major training agreements with national companies, including IBM; Flexographic Technical Association; Inter-Industry Conference on Auto Collision Repair (I-CAR); AutoCAD; Blackhawk; Kansas Jack; Weinig; and Food, Machinery, and Chemicals (FMC).

A customer suggestion system has been established to ensure an easy avenue for customers to comment, seek assistance, or call attention to problems with instruction and service. Additionally, students evaluate instruction at least once during each course. A college-wide survey is conducted regularly in order to solicit student opinions in four categories:

1. Methods of instruction and equipment

2. Teaching effectiveness

3. Core services used by most students

4. Other support services

Figure 9.6 lists the results of student ratings of teaching effectiveness as reported in the student satisfaction survey which was conducted in May 1990.

| Item | Mean | % Of Those Responding | | | | | Percent |
		VD(1)	SD(2)	N(3)	SS(4)	VS(5)	Responding
Follows up on Questions	4.23	-%	4%	12%	40%	44%	100%
States Expectations	4.16	-%	3%	13%	48%	36%	99%
Uses Appropriate Resources	4.13	1%	3%	15%	46%	36%	99%
Follows Curriculum	4.11	1%	3%	13%	50%	33%	99%
Starts & Ends Class on Time	4.10	2%	6%	15%	37%	41%	100%
Assists in Achieving Goals	4.09	1%	5%	15%	41%	38%	99%
Provides Reinforcement	4.01	1%	5%	18%	42%	33%	100%
Provide Opportunities for Success	4.00	1%	5%	19%	45%	31%	99%
Seeks Feedback	3.90	1%	6%	21%	45%	27%	99%
Encourages Alternate Ways for Tasks	3.83	1%	4%	27%	46%	22%	98%
Reduces Anxiety	3.47	5%	11%	34%	34%	17%	99%

1=Very Dissatisfied   3=Neither Satisfied Nor Dissatisfied   5=Very Satisfied
2=Somewhat Dissatisfied   4=Somewhat Satisfied

Figure 9.6 – Summary of Ratings of Teaching Effectiveness Based on Student Satisfaction Survey Results

	1985	1986	1987	1988	1989	Change
Accepts Responsibility	4.28	4.24	4.21	4.20	4.29	+0.01
Cooperates with Co-workers	4.33	4.36	4.26	4.33	4.37	+0.04
Has Good Work Attendance	4.48	4.51	4.48	4.51	4.52	+0.04
Accepts Advice and Supervision	4.27	4.36	4.29	4.23	4.29	+0.02
Desires to Learn and Improve	4.34	4.39	4.35	4.31	4.34	—
Completes Work on Time	4.14	4.17	4.18	4.15	4.13	-0.01
Practices Good Safety Habits	4.16	4.23	4.23	4.20	4.13	-0.03
Displays Good Work Attitude	4.24	4.35	4.32	4.23	4.29	+0.05

5 = Excellent, 4 = Good, 3 = Average, 2 = Poor, 1 = Very Poor

Figure 9.7 – Employer Satisfaction Survey Results

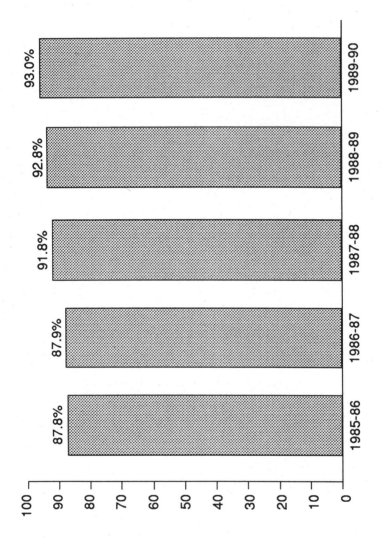

Figure 9.8 – Graduate Placement Results

Several other surveys have been conducted to measure satisfaction by customers other than students. One deals with employer satisfaction with graduates (Figure 9.7). The school also conducts follow-up studies to determine placement of graduates and starting salaries. There has been improvement in placement as shown in Figure 9.8.

A Customer Service Committee at the college has developed conforming requirements for the customer service quality element. These are monitored during the program and service audits.

The district has two policies that deal with providing guarantees to customers. The first is a retraining guarantee (refer to Figure 2.3) and the second is a satisfaction guarantee for business and industry who contract with the college (refer to Figure 2.2). In addition to the satisfaction policies, a success profile has been established by a faculty/staff committee to assist incoming students. These "guidelines for success" are outlined in a brochure which is given to students when they enroll.

Customer complaints are handled quickly. When conditions or procedures under the control of the college are the source of the complaint, refunds are given. The college has not yet established written policies or procedures for handling complaints; however, this is planned for next year together with formal training in customer service improvement for all staff and student workers.

Several FVTC programs as well as staff and students have received national awards. The college, in 1985, was selected by the American Vocational Association as one of the top three post-secondary occupational colleges in the country. The school also received two national leadership awards in 1990, one from the American Society for Training and Development (ASTD) and the other from the Association of Community College Trustees (ACCT). The Wood Technics program was selected as the top vocational program in Wisconsin in 1990. In 1991, the college was chosen as a "National Exemplary College" by the National Center for Vocational Education in Los Angeles. As a result, the school will be used by the Center to develop a graduate leadership course.

There have been significant increases in enrollments the past few years. Figure 9.9 shows that there have been steady increases in enrollments in all target markets, with a major increase in business and industry enrollments.

Customer satisfaction continues to be a major initiative of the quality improvement process at the college. Major focus has been placed on improving relationships with internal (coworkers) and external (students, employers, and taxpayers) customers. Special training in customer service is being provided to all service departments and support staff. In addition, a staff member has been appointed to manage customer service at the college and to provide assistance to staff in improving services to customers.

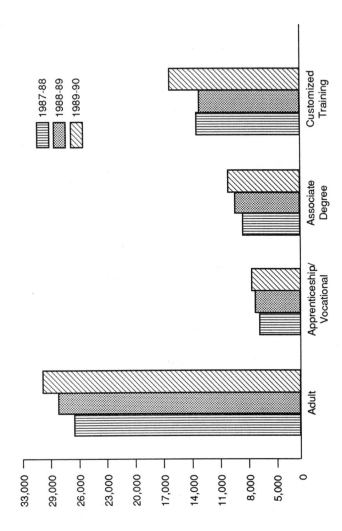

Figure 9.9 – Enrollment Increases at FVTC for 1987–1990

Some Reflections And Thoughts On Application

Since the quality initiative began at FVTC, we have patiently waited for concrete examples of increased productivity and reduced costs. As the chief executive officer of the college, I am held accountable to the board of education for new projects and initiatives, including the quality improvement process.

Although W. Edwards Deming contends that the process, by its very nature, will produce positive results, it's necessary to have evidence to substantiate its existence and continuation. That's why we instituted a comprehensive research/evaluation system that includes measures from several surveys and audits. The results have been mixed, but there have been many positive indicators of success.

What's difficult to determine is which success stories of the college should be attributed to the quality process and which would have occurred without it. Since the college has had an excellent reputation and has generally been looked upon as innovative and progressive, many positive things may have happened anyhow just because of the expertise and creativity of the faculty and staff.

However, the research/evaluation system shows many positive results that can be attributed directly to the quality initiative. The majority of these success indicators have been reported in the Malcolm Baldrige examination responses. Many other positive occurrences are probably the result of the process, but it could be argued otherwise.

For example, the Faculty Union agreed on a three-year contract in 1990, the first of that length in the history of the school. Likewise, a four-year contract was reached with support staff, another first for the college. Also, in 1989-90, the number of grievances was down signifi-cantly and there have been much better relations with the two unions.

Other positive impacts because of quality include:

- Increased credibility with business and industry

- Improved marketing image to prospective students

- Approval of an associate degree program in quality

- Increased enrollments

- Recognition for leadership and innovation

- Better increased placement rates

Of course, I'm biased toward the quality improvement process since it began under my leadership. Because I'm looking at things more positively, things may look better than they really are. On the other hand, because there are those who would like to see the quality initiative disappear, I try to make sure that any claims of success are substantiated with valid data.

Many people feel good about this growth at FVTC. It makes the staff proud to be singled out as the first public school in the country to adopt a business approach to education.

Summary

There is enough evidence of success with the quality process at FVTC to warrant optimism about its potential to impact positively on education overall. Several indicators show positive improvement in key areas of the college. This chapter highlights those successes and uses data to illustrate improvement.

There is strong evidence to support the notion that the quality process, to be successful, requires a major commitment by school personnel. Since every process comes under review, strong leadership at all levels of the organization is required.

This chapter identified strengths of the college and several areas that have been targeted for improvement. Improvement is needed in communications and in the integration of statistical thinking approaches into problem-solving and overall school evaluation processes. There is also a need for specialized staff training.

Several approaches have been used by the college in the research and evaluation model that has been adopted. Customer satisfaction and employee surveys are being conducted and most have been positive. The use of the Malcolm Baldrige examination criteria has enhanced the evaluation system.

CHAPTER 10

THE NEVER-ENDING JOURNEY— WHAT HAPPENS NEXT?

As stated throughout this book, the quality process, properly applied, has the potential to positively change American schools. It provides the framework and the systematic approach to examine all management and technical processes, transactions, services, and teaching activities. It has an accountability component that demands that the establishment of criteria (conforming requirements) be based on customer expectations. The goal is to continue to improve until customer expectations are met and exceeded.

Conforming requirements, which provide the criteria for the quality elements, form the basis for self-analyses, reviews, audits, evaluations, and other types of measurements. Using statistical thinking approaches and techniques, careful monitoring of variability is beginning to occur. Problem solving at the lowest level in the organization is encouraged.

All this leads to new ways and different structures to operate schools. The breakdown of hierarchical, bureaucratic organizations is promoted, and the improvement of the overall school climate is encouraged.

Decision making is advocated at the levels closest to the customers. As a result, teachers and support staff assume key roles in the management of schools.

Some sort of plan is required to make this all happen. It doesn't matter which quality model is selected since they all provide a sequential approach to improvement. Eventually, each school will probably decide on the model that best fits the personality and uniqueness of the staff. Several common key elements are essential and the ones selected at FVTC have been highlighted throughout this book.

After six challenging years of implementation, the never-ending journey toward quality improvement goes onward at FVTC. Each new year brings renewed excitement that is tempered by the realization that organization-wide improvement is also never-ending. As more faculty and staff embrace the concept, success will become more apparent and the effectiveness of the college will continue to improve. The future is encouraging...the outlook is positive...the commitment is growing stronger.

Emerging are new paradigms that create shifts in ways to do things. These new concepts are impacting all areas of the school. They are being created even though the old ways are relatively successful. The paradigm pioneers who had the courage and creativity to explore new ways to do things have relished the risk-taking atmosphere which exists in the college. A list of the paradigm shifts for each step of the Fox Valley Model is found in Appendices S through V.

Many of these ideas were rejected initially and some are still being challenged by those who hesitate to try new paradigms. Some have failed completely. These opposing forces—those staff who pioneer innovation and those who resist change—create special challenges for managers. In most cases, parallel structures are required to support the new ideas while the old paradigms are still in place. This perpetual process requires creative leadership with the skills to deal with this dichotomy of balancing skills and resources with the old and the new. The result of it all leads to educational change that is dynamic and futuristic.

The successful management of these paradigm shifts leads to excellence in education. The change process that encourages debate and risk taking is healthy for any school. At FVTC the quality improvement process has been used to keep that momentum going.

New paradigms have resulted in pioneering by faculty and staff in the seven areas that are grouped under the umbrella of quality elements. These elements, together with their conforming requirements, have fostered new and successful ways to educate students and manage the college. These paradigm shifts are at various stages of maturity because the process continues to foster new ideas that will lead to further innovation and improvement.

Yet, it is essential that we continue to establish goals and identify challenges that lie ahead. We must look to our strengths and weaknesses from the past and build on them in the years ahead.

In July 1990, a team of faculty and staff met in a retreat to continue this type of planning. They met to identify our thrusts for the future. These ideas are summarized below by Carol Tyler, former teacher, quality coordinator, and now trainer/consultant for The Academy for Quality in Education.

Where Do We Go From Here?

One of the ironies of a quality improvement process is that not only are services and products being continuously improved, but the process itself is also continuously improved. Two years into implementation of the process, we made changes in the process itself. Four years into implementation, we are again about to make changes.

The five full years of implementation of the quality process at FVTC have been rich in experience. The obstacles to process success that were once imagined are now known. Strategies designed to change organizational culture and to improve the delivery of products and services have proven successful or unsuccessful and the reasons for the success or lack thereof are understood. We are at a crossroads. We know that quality improvement is a workable and worthwhile effort in our school, and we now have the experience to make it a more effective effort.

Two years ago we made changes in our quality process model by adding and deleting steps in the model. The changes we now propose may not result in changes in the model. Rather, they are changes in how well or fully we implement the steps of the model and in how well we integrate these steps with each other and with the mission and daily operations of the school.

The changes that are proposed are based on a variety of input. Input from external customers came in the form of our Student Satisfaction Survey and from data on student placement and employer satisfaction. Input from internal customers came in the form of the Organizational Climate Survey and the study on the availability of time as a resource. In addition, specific feedback on the focus of the quality effort over the next few years was sought from the Quality Process Audit, from The Academy for Quality in Education, and from the TQLC.

The information and impressions provided by these varied sources showed some definite similarities. From these similarities, our future quality improvement focus was formed. Our future directions in improving our processes, products, and services are as follows:

Improve Communication

I once heard a communications consultant advise an audience to spend an entire year developing a communications system and excellent communications skills before embarking on a quality improvement effort. There is more to this advice than a shrewd attempt to bolster the communications consultancy business.

Because of the cultural upheaval involved in a quality improvement process, good communication is critical. We need good communication processes and systems and the skills to use them well. We will renew our efforts to improve every aspect of communication at FVTC, internal and external.

Determine Customer Requirements

This most basic of concepts in the quality revolution can prove deceptively simple. Many of us thought we were already close to the customer and knew customer requirements. We now understand that the effort to determine, review, and evaluate those requirements must be systematic. Employees need assistance in how to do that. We plan to provide it.

Provide Adequate and Ongoing Facilitation for Process Improvement Activities

Problem solving and process improvement through the application of a formal problem-solving process or scientific method is the crux of an improvement effort. We now see that these efforts must have, at least initially, outside facilitation. This applies to work groups, to cross-functional teams, and to special task forces. Formal improvement efforts will be launched across the board as a result of management training in statistical thinking, and support of these efforts will be provided by trained facilitators.

Focus on a Few Priorities Throughout the Organization

This reflects two themes that arose repeatedly. One is to integrate quality into the planning process or to better demonstrate how the quality improvement effort supports the mission of the school. The other is to focus our organizational goals and improvement activities on a few areas and to ensure that these goals are clearly understood by everyone in the organization.

Make Involvement in the Quality Improvement Process a Positive Experience

The Quality Audit Team went so far as to suggest that we make quality improvement "fun." My recent experience facilitating a problem-solving activity convinced me that this is not a frivolous suggestion. Much work was accomplished and much laughter was heard. We need to offer the quality process as a helpful tool to employees. We need to allow them to see the rewards to their customers and themselves. We need to recognize their efforts. We need to personalize the process.

Provide Education

One of the most stinging comments from the Quality Process Audit suggested that while FVTC is excellent at educating students, we have ignored the desperate cries for training of our own staff. We have made tremendous efforts in this area through the appointment of a training director and through increases in the training budget. These efforts will be intensified.

Provide Time to Do the Job Right

The clearly stated staff need for more time will be addressed. This need was demonstrated by the time study to be present in every level of the organization and in every department. Just as the quality process was brought to bear on faculty and support staff negotiations this last year, so will it be brought to bear on this issue. The first step is the Conflict Resolution Workshop in August 1990 jointly hosted and participated by union and management.

Perhaps this list does not appear to be singular in any way. Most of these steps appeared in our original quality process model and then again in our revised model. So what is different about listing them now? The list is not different, but those writing it and reading it are. Marcel Proust wrote, "The real voyage of discovery lies not in seeking new lands but in seeing with new eyes."

We see the above "to do" list with new eyes. We better understand the need for each item on the list and the complexity of implementation. This is our list, not the list of a guru, and we discovered it on our own. Of more importance, we got to know each other and the shared problems of the organization along the way. In the spirit of continuous improvement, we welcome the challenges brought by these areas of focus as we will welcome the list after this one.

Carol Tyler

APPENDIX A

LONG-RANGE QUALITY GOALS 1985–1990

Written in November 1985

The overriding goal is for all people to view FVTC as a high-quality, post-secondary institution. This will be accomplished by the initiation of a "Quality First" process which has a goal of "Guaranteed Customer Satisfaction" as evidenced by these features which will be in place no later than 1990:

1. Conscientious employees with attitudes and motivation to foster and maintain a quality atmosphere in all departments of the college. This involves:

   a. Attracting, selecting, and keeping quality employees.

   b. Establishing a "customer first" attitude in all departments of the college.

   c. Making decisions within a specific area following maximum input by the affected employees.

   d. Encouraging continued employee innovation and flexibility to cope with technological changes.

   e. Creating a "Zero Errors" program with the goal of eliminating all errors in all products and services.

2. Students and graduates will be completely satisfied with their experiences in instructional programs and courses as evidenced by the following "Guaranteed Satisfaction" features:

   a. The goal of each degree and diploma program will be job placement for each person who successfully completes the graduation requirements. This will involve:

      1) Ensuring that we operate an exemplary career planning and counseling service that assists students in making wise career choices.

      2) Establishing prerequisites for students so that they have the necessary background to successfully complete the program.

3) Ensuring the existence of a strong developmental education department to help students who have basic skills deficiencies meet program entry requirements.

4) Developing curricula based on measurable performance objectives and competencies that are tied to jobs for which we train.

5) Designing evaluation for each performance objective so that students know what they must do to meet program requirements.

6) Intensifying the Instructional Audit System to ensure rapid feedback when the program placement rates fall below the ideal goal of 100 percent placement.

3. A guaranteed satisfaction plan will be instituted in college programs to provide assurance that each student's expectations will be fulfilled. This will involve:

a. Carefully defining what is to be taught in each course through the establishment of performance-based course objectives.

b. Determining what each student expects from the course and preparing written agreements accordingly.

c. Establishing student requirements related to attendance, assignments, and other factors related to student success.

d. Changing the Wisconsin Administrative Rules to permit guaranteed satisfaction paybacks to those who do not meet these objectives.

A SUMMARY OF THE FVTC QUALITY FIRST PROCESS MODEL

1. Demonstrate Management Commitment

Management has the power to make decisions that will create a quality organization. Their commitment must be assured first so that they can be role models for other employees and so that they will create a quality environment for employees to enter after training.

2. Establish a Total Quality Leadership Council

A Total Quality Leadership Council needs to be established very early to define the process and to develop its framework. This council then sets the process in motion and continues to monitor it. Membership of the council should include a cross-section of the organization.

3. Determine the Cost of Quality

The quality movement was born out of a need to stay financially competitive. Careful determination and continual monitoring of the cost of quality is essential to the process, providing a critical measure of its success.

4. Provide Education and Training

All members of the organization need to be educated in the background of the quality movement and the fundamentals of a quality improvement process. Equally important, employees will also need training in the skills required to implement a process successfully—communication, problem solving, teamwork.

5. Identify Roles and Establish Performance Requirements

Employees need an opportunity to identify their role in the process so that they can immediately begin to implement quality in their day-to-day work. Old requirements need to be reviewed in the context of the organization's quality process, and new requirements need to be established.

6. Implement a Quality Communication System

Communication, always critical, becomes even more so in the midst of widespread organizational change. The effort to communicate information about the quality process must be comprehensive and sustained. The organization should analyze its existing communication system to ensure that it can meet this requirement.

7. Measure and Set Goals

Quality theorists offer a variety of approaches to measurement, but all agree that continuous measurement is essential. Goals should be set, based on measurement. Measurement should be used to determine whether goals are reached—a continuous cycle.

8. Identify and Eliminate Problems

For the improvement process to work, obstacles to getting the job done right the first time must be removed. A climate that encourages the identification of obstacles and insists upon their removal must be established. A mechanism to make it happen must be developed.

9. Research and Develop New Initiatives

Research is the foundation for planning and prevention. The organization needs to keep up with developments in the application of quality theory, as well as developments in the delivery of products and services relevant to the organization.

10. Create a Structure for Employee Involvement

An opportunity for every employee to participate in the quality improvement process must be provided. A primary strategy to achieve participation is the establishment of teams.

11. Establish Accountability

Accountability is absolutely essential! Valid requirements that have been agreed upon and articulated must be met every time. Personal and process accountability procedures need to be developed and strictly adhered to.

12. Launch a Customer Revolution

Every successful quality improvement process has at its heart an obsession with customer satisfaction. The efforts of every employee must be ultimately targeted at establishing, meeting, or exceeding customer requirements.

13. Recognize, Reward, and Celebrate

Quality happens when people make it happen. The people who make it happen, individually and in teams, should be generously recognized and appropriately rewarded. Their successes should be joyously celebrated!

14. Conduct Quality Audits

An independent audit of the process is essential. Internal measures will provide information on the success of the process. An external audit will provide an additional, crucial perspective.

15. Link to the Community

A quality process, developed and implemented with the understanding and support of local business, industry, education, and government, has a greatly increased chance of succeeding. At the very least, communication about quality with these groups needs to be established and maintained. Wherever possible, partnerships in quality need to be established and nurtured.

16. Strive for Continuous Improvement

The commitment to a quality approach to doing business involves an endorsement of the philosophy "If it works, make it better." The process is never-ending. It is endlessly adaptable to changing technology and a shifting marketplace.

ROLES OF THOSE INVOLVED IN TEAMS

Quality Facilitator's Role

1. Keep the process moving

   a. Definition of team

   b. Establishment of communication system

   c. Identification and selection of obstacle

   d. Application of problem-solving process

2. Inform, support, help, and coach the team

3. Listen to team members

4. Provide opportunities for team member involvement

5. Communicate with the team, supervisor, and quality coordinator

6. Act as the "hub"

7. Make sure problem-solving activities are discussed

8. Lead discussion of problem-solving activities at work unit meetings

9. Keep a log of activities

10. Write final report

11. Maintain and promote a positive attitude

12. Maintain visibility of process

13. Establish time line and meet deadlines

Immediate Supervisor's Role

1. Support and encourage the team, facilitator, and process

2. Provide resources

3. Integrate activities into planning/budgeting process

4 Provide communication paths within the organization

5. Participate

6. Provide guidance/direction...but not too much

7. Recognize efforts and progress

8. Promote positive attitude/approach to activities

Role of the Measurement Consultant

1. Be a resource: provide information, tools, techniques, methods

2. Be a sounding board: review, critique process, approach, advise

3. Train the facilitator/team

4. Link team to other resources in the school

Role of Team Members

1. Cooperate

2. Provide input and output/participate

3. Support facilitator and process activities

4. Communicate

5. Commit

6. Compromise

7. Be open-minded

8. Assist with every step (see list above)

Quality Coordinator's Role

1. Monitor progress of teams

2. Act as clearinghouse

3. Collect and disseminate information on progress of teams

4. Provide resources, information, training

5. Provide direction

6. Provide support

7. Advocate implementation of team solutions/recommendations

8. Provide time schedules; be a prompter

9. Advocate team resources, allocate time

10. Link with the TQLC

Appendix D

A Union Perspective on Quality

Yvonne Matz, Educational Support Personnel Association President, and Ron Toshner, Faculty Association President

As FVTC began developing the quality process, the faculty and support personnel unions became involved in the early stages. The initial reactions from staff ranged from "This is just another fad" to "Let's give it a try." Since the history of the staff/administration relationship did not support the level of trust necessary for success, the unions' leadership, as well as the administration, believed that full communications between staff and administration would be essential for the success of this venture. Thus, the parties began this venture with some misgivings but with the hope that positive results would be achieved.

Over the next several years as the quality process developed at FVTC, the unions' leadership began to see some of those positive changes they desired. Communications did indeed improve. There was much less hesitancy for the administration and union leadership to discuss issues affecting the staff and the college. That improved communication brought about an improved attitude—there was more of a desire to resolve problems, to find solutions, to reduce the level of confrontation that existed in the past. Overall, the unions and the administration began more shared decision making to reach mutually satisfying solutions.

But was everything going smoothly? Were there questions about the effectiveness of the process? Unfortunately, there were some problems. One of the greatest frustrations experienced was the perceived and/or real lack of total commitment from some staff—management, faculty, and support personnel. From the unions' viewpoint, some management supported the quality process in words but not in actions. Not all faculty and support staff were willing to give the process a chance. As a result, the union leadership felt that the commitment to quality, the change of the work environment, was moving far too slowly. In fact, the union leadership felt that at times FVTC was emphasizing the *process* as if it were a separate activity rather than a change of attitude that permeates all activities. Thus, the negative feelings stemmed not from a

169

disenchantment with the idea of quality but rather from the slowness of the implementation.

As quality matures at FVTC, the union leadership sees communication between administration and the FVTC board becoming even more open. The old viewpoint of taking sides on an issue needs to be downplayed and the belief that mutual problem solving is most beneficial to all those involved needs to become dominant. The commitment to quality *must* move from a commitment of words to active involvement by staff. The "quality *process*" should actually disappear at FVTC. In essence, quality must become a "way of life" for every staff member at FVTC, not just an activity done at a certain time and then set aside.

APPENDIX E

QUALITY ELEMENT
HUMAN RESOURCES

Quality Element – Human Resources

Each FVTC employee is a valuable resource to the organization. FVTC will work with all employees to enable them to meet the preestablished requirements for their jobs. Employees at all levels will be provided the opportunity to interact with each other in such a way that mutual respect for one another and for the organization is achieved.

FVTC provides a quality work environment which is supportive of people doing their jobs right the first time in meeting the educational and service needs of their customers. The organizational climate fosters an attitude of respect for one another and provides opportunities to maximize every employee's potential. Such an environment is safe, clean, technologically current, comfortable, and attractive for educational and administrative functions.

FVTC employees are expected to display behavior that creates a positive attitude, enthusiasm, loyalty, and a commitment to the goals, the objectives, and the mission of the institution. Employee commitment, dedication, and hard work will, in turn, enable the college to meet its goals, objectives, and mission.

Conforming Requirements	Measurement Strategy	Cost of Nonconformance
1. Employees meet the minimum qualifications for the position they currently hold. Qualifications for each position are periodically reviewed and updated as duties and responsibilities change.	Instructional Audits Certification Audits Performance Management Evaluation	Certification audit exception Lost labor and productivity Cost of reclassification
2. Professional growth, career planning, and promotional preparedness opportunities are clearly defined. Information and support are made available to employees. A professional development plan exists for each employee in the organization.	Instructional Audits Professional Growth Budget Performance Management Evaluation Professional Growth Plan	Program discontinuance Decrease in productivity of individual
3. All recruitment, written materials, media materials, and human interaction are free of discrimination. Handicapped employees are able to gain access, without restriction, to physical facilities, and physical facilities meet all state and local requirements.	Affirmative Action Plan Instructional Audit North Central Evaluation	Loss of federal monies and student financial aid due to not meeting certain mandated requirements, if found to be discriminatory Poor public relations Higher employee turnover Student costs Employer costs

Conforming Requirements	Measurement Strategy	Cost of Nonconformance
4. Employment practices provide equal opportunities for applicants and promotion of employees.	Affirmative Action Annual Report	Loss of Federal monies due to not meeting certain mandated requirements and student financial aid, if found to be discriminatory Poor public relations
5. Recognition of an employee whose efforts meet and/or exceed the job requirements is immediate, individual, and flexible.	Performance Management Evaluation Climate survey; several questions address this issue Recognition Plan	Decrease in productivity of individual Loss of feeling of being part of the organization Higher employee turnover
6. The work environment reflects the college's mission with emphasis on the adult learner.	North Central Evaluation Student Satisfaction Survey Organizational Climate Survey	Lowered community image Loss of FTEs Increase in dropouts Lower enrollments
7. Employee work space is attractive and is: – professionally designed and maintained – appealing to the needs of the customers – color-coordinated and aesthetically compatible with surroundings	Organizational Climate Survey Instructional Audit	Personnel Problems: Morale – Counseling Physical – Insurance Costs Absenteeism Higher employee costs of recruitment and training
8. An ongoing safety inspection is conducted by a college safety committee to identify potential problems.	North Central Evaluation Accident Reports Attendance Records	Employee absence due to accidents Insurance costs Worker compensation
9. Employees display initiative on the job that includes suggesting new ideas to improve personal and/or FVTC performance and job satisfaction.	The number of ideas/suggestions that employees make via evaluation or suggestion box. We need to encourage this creativity to happen.	Employee morale suffers Higher employee turnover

Conforming Requirements	Measurement Strategy	Cost of Nonconformance
10. Flexibility which includes the ability and willingness to readily accept and adapt to changes in procedures or assignments is shown by employees.	Climate Survey Student Evaluation of Instruction Performance Evaluation	Absenteeism Punctuality Internal and external customer dissatisfaction
11. Employees have a positive attitude and enthusiasm on the job, including cooperation with all other employees, customers, and the general public, and working toward the implementation of goals and policies with an openness to constructive criticism.	Organizational Climate Survey; this will give an indication, but will not measure directly. Could test new hires via Testing Center. Student Evaluation of Instruction	Decrease in productivity of individual and team Absenteeism Punctuality
12. Employees display the ability to effectively communicate—listen, understand, and be understood both in written and oral communication, and to express themselves in a positive manner.	Evidence of teamwork communication in climate for work group area	Decrease in productivity of individual and team Organizational confusion
13. Managers actively promote teamwork and problem solving within their immediate unit and beyond in order to develop higher levels of job satisfaction and esprit de corps.	Organizational Climate Survey Performance Evaluation Student Satisfaction Survey	Decrease in productivity of individual and team Loss of FTEs Customer dissatisfaction Morale problems

APPENDIX F

QUALITY ELEMENT
CURRICULUM AND INSTRUCTION

Quality Element – Curriculum and Instruction

The purpose of FVTC's curriculum is to prepare individuals for success in the world of work, both now and in the future. Our broad-based, flexible curriculum format provides an overall instructional strategy for developing each individual learner's potential from the most basic skill level to the most highly technical.

The goal is to have each program course developed into a complete plan for instruction with measurable objectives geared toward helping the individual master a set of specific, relevant competencies that are based on the current and future requirements of the workplace.

FVTC offers a variety of scheduling options to serve the growing need for flexibility in providing training at nontraditional times. In this multiple entry/exit approach, individuals may enter programs and courses at a variety of times throughout the year, rather than only at traditional fall or spring times, and may graduate with the same flexibility during the year.

In recognizing the variety of students' learning styles, as well as the variety of instructional styles within the instructional process, FVTC supports competency-based instruction utilizing current technology both in the traditional group-based setting and in independent self-paced study.

The curriculum and instructional process also involves a deep commitment to the economic development of the business community. In partnership with business and industry, FVTC offers customized training and retraining.

Since the instructional process revolves around the individual student, FVTC offers a variety of services to meet a variety of needs. Providing appropriate services to support students during the educational process is essential for their success. Therefore, prospective students, both full- and part-time, may take advantage of group and/or individual career and program counseling and assessment throughout the calendar year. Students who do not meet the minimum math and reading requirements set by programs must complete appropriate GOAL courses. Additional counseling is available to identify and serve the needs of the traditional, nontraditional, and special needs students throughout their school careers, including a spectrum of job placement activities before and after graduation.

Conforming Requirements	Measurement Strategy	Cost of Nonconformance
1. There is a complete plan for learning for each course in a program, and the computer is used as a tool to maintain a master file in a central location. (See policy – Curriculum Documentation/Curriculum Assessment form)	Instructional Audit North Central Evaluation	Student costs Rework when revising curriculum
a. Curriculum is based on competencies needed for the person to perform successfully on the job.	Instructional Audit Employer Survey North Central Evaluation	Student and employer costs
b. Course prerequisites are clearly defined.	Program Development State Regulations Program Revision State Regulations North Central Evaluation	Student costs Loss of FTEs

Conforming Requirements	Measurement Strategy	Cost of Nonconformance
c. Curriculum and course requirements are consistent for content, textbook, materials/tools and grading policy. Exceptions must be approved by the dean of the division.	Student Satisfaction Survey	Student costs
d. Students may receive advanced standing and/or credit for past experiences in education in occupations related to the program.	Instructional Audit Student Satisfaction Survey *Counselor Survey (formal mechanism not in place)	Student costs
e. An optimum class size is established for each course.	Instructional Audit Student Satisfaction Survey	Student costs
f. There is a plan in each division to evaluate curriculum and instruction. (See Human Resources Conforming Requirements)	Instructional Audit *(Needs additional measurement activities) Student Survey	Student costs Taxpayer costs
g. Examinations have criteria with a direct link to the performance objectives.	Instructional Audit	Employer costs
2. Programs are structured to permit multiple-entry and multiple-exit.	Instructional Audit Utilization Reports North Central Evaluation	Student Station Occupancy Ratios
3 Instructors use industry standard technology placing emphasis on leading edge technology as identified by advisory committee. (See Use of Technology #8)	Instructional Audit Employer Survey Placement Records	Student and employer costs
4. All courses in full-time programs have some high-technology components which require students to use computers regularly. (See Use of Technology #9)	Instructional Audit Employer Survey	Student and employer costs

Conforming Requirements	Measurement Strategy	Cost of Nonconformance
5. Each program will provide some type of work experience related to the student's training.	Instructional Audit North Central Evaluation	Student and employer costs
6. Instructors use a variety of teaching techniques to meet the unique needs of the learner.	Instructional Audit Student Satisfaction Survey	Student costs
7. Faculty assess students' needs, determine strengths and weaknesses, prescribe learning paths for students, and make appropriate referrals to improve the retention of students.	Instructional Audit Student Withdrawal Report	Student costs Loss of FTEs
8. Services to support student success are accessible and effective.	Student Satisfaction Survey	Student costs Loss of FTEs
9. Curriculum and instruction is customized for individual businesses to assist them with their productivity and profitability.	Requirements of customer contract Instructional Audit	Employer costs Retraining costs
10. There are formal articulation and/or transfer credit agreements with area secondary and postsecondary schools for each program.	Instructional Audit North Central Evaluation	Student costs Taxpayer costs
11. Students are aware of expectations for each course through a syllabus, grading policy, attendance, and safety requirements.	*No measurement in place at this time. Will be a unit objective for next year	Student costs
12. Student organizations are available for those who wish to participate.	Instructional Audits Student Satisfaction Survey	Loss of FTEs
13. Each program advisory committee is comprised of an equal number of employees and employers and meets at least twice a year regarding curriculum, equipment, facilities, staffing, and other related activities.	Instructional Audit North Central Evaluation Minutes sent to Vice President of Academic Affairs	Retraining costs

Conforming Requirements	Measurement Strategy	Cost of Nonconformance
14. Instructors conform to established time lines. a. Classes start and end on time. b. Grades are submitted promptly.	Student Satisfaction Survey	Student costs
	*Needs development of measurement strategy.	

APPENDIX G

QUALITY ELEMENT
GOAL SETTING

Quality Element – Goal Setting

FVTC uses a strategic planning process which encourages and provides opportunities for participation at all levels in the organization to include both short- and long-range plans that are consistent with the directions of the institution. Planning is used as the cornerstone for establishing goals, operational plans, and individual management objectives with research being used to solidify that framework. An important factor is the necessity to link the strategic planning process with the operational and budgetary process. The purpose of this linkage is to properly reflect resource allocation.

Conforming Requirements	Measurement Strategy	Cost of Nonconformance
1. The college's current mission and purpose are clearly stated without ambiguous or confusing jargon.	FVTC Board Approval Documentation of Review Plan	District resources may be used for inappropriate activities
2. There is a written 3-year operational plan which contains strategic directions, and includes the following elements: – Goal Setting – Human Resources – Curriculum and Instruction – Use of Technology – Marketing – Customer Service – Quality-Based Manager	Approval of Executive Cabinet Documentation of Review Plan Instructional Audit	District resources may be used for inappropriate activities
3. The needs of external customers are identified, prioritized, and used to provide direction for the organization/program/department.	Advisory Committee Minutes Instructional Audits Program Approval Employer Survey	High-cost, low-enrollment programs, and customer complaints where customer needs are not being met Employer costs Loss of community support

Conforming Requirements	Measurement Strategy	Cost of Nonconformance
4. Individuals at all levels in the organization are involved in the planning process.	Climate Survey Employee Satisfaction Survey Instructional Audits Advisory Committee Minutes North Central Evaluation	Poor staff morale, lack of support and commitment to the organization Increased grievances and labor unrest Higher FTE costs Poor customer service
5. Communication on operational planning is ongoing and flows upward, downward, and across the organization.	Climate Survey Instructional Audits North Central Evaluation Advisory Committee Minutes	Higher FTE costs Poor customer service
6. The operational plan is the basis for the development of the budget.	Annual Budget Instructional Audits	Goals and objectives in operational plan not met Poor employee morale Lack of customer satisfaction
7. The planning process is continuous (year-round) and flexible to allow the organization to be dynamic and responsive.	Budget Allocations Staff Satisfaction Survey Instructional Audits North Central Evaluation	Higher student dropout rates Poor employee morale Higher employee turnover

APPENDIX H

QUALITY ELEMENT
USE OF TECHNOLOGY

Quality Element – Use of Technology

Comprehensive use of technology is required at all levels at FVTC. Relying on an effective system of technology use, competency-based instruction allows students to enroll continuously in a perpetual enrollment and graduation system and permits students to proceed through instruction at a pace considered consistent with their past experiences. Technology is used to assist in the management and instruction programs. Information processing systems which include functions related to instruction, administration, and office computing are a part of everyday life.

Conforming Requirements	Measurement Strategy	Cost of Nonconformance
1. Management units use technology and support services to effectively manage and produce concise reports, documents, communications, and schedules.	Survey staff to find out if they: Are receiving the reports they need to manage effectively Are getting the reports in a timely manner Are using the reports to guide their action Ensure that internally generated reports and communications are concise Insist on short memos (no more than one page) Conduct interviews of staff to determine needs	Paper costs Employee costs of meetings where lengthy reports are presented Costs of handling, reading, storing, etc., excessively long documents
2. Through the use of electronic data generation and on-line view capabilities, hard copy documentation is significantly reduced.	Measure volume of paper used (should show minimum of 10% decrease during first full year) Survey staff to determine: Extent of electronic system use Possible improvements	Paper cost Costs of handling and storing hard copy documents

Conforming Requirements	Measurement Strategy	Cost of Nonconformance
3. Service and support units use technology to manage their processes effectively and productively.	Determine processes to be automated Measure progress being made toward automation Conduct study to determine extent of use in each department	Employee costs of continuing to do things manually Cost of productivity decline
4. Instructional managers use media and information processing systems to effectively support faculty with the instructional process.	Determine processes to be automated Measure progress being made toward automation Climate Survey Conduct study to determine extent of use in each department	Lost employee productivity
5. Technology is used to effectively assist in the teaching and management of instructional programs offered under the perpetual enrollment/graduation process.	North Central Evaluation Student Station Occupancy Withdrawal Reports Graduate Follow Up Student Evaluation of Instruction	Lost FTEs Cost of idle student workstations Cost of student noncompletion Cost of poor institutional image
6. Courses use technology to assist faculty with computer-based testing, drill-and-practice tutorial education, and other computer-based education components.	Instructional Audit Student Satisfaction Survey Student time on computer reports Advisory Committee's Review Curriculum Design Review	Employer costs of additional training Cost of lost economic development contracts Cost of lost FTEs Cost of retraining Cost of poor institutional image
7. Instructional management employs central computerized record-keeping systems to monitor student progress and performance.	Instructional Audit Survey of Students Survey of Staff	Student costs Cost of poor institutional image

Conforming Requirements	Measurement Strategy	Cost of Nonconformance
8. Instructors use industry standard technology placing emphasis on leading-edge technology as identified by advisory committees. (See Curriculum and Instruction #3)	Instructional Audit Employers Survey Graduate Follow Up Advisory Committees	Employer costs of additional training Cost of lost economic development contracts Cost of lost FTEs Cost of retraining Cost of poor institutional image
9. All courses in full-time programs have some high technology components which require students to use computers regularly. (See Curriculum and Instruction #4)	Instructional Audit Student Evaluation of Instruction Advisory Committee's Review	Employer costs of additional training Cost of lost economic development contracts Cost of lost FTEs Cost of retraining Cost of poor institutional image

APPENDIX I

QUALITY ELEMENT
MARKETING

Quality Element – Marketing

The FVTC marketing process aligns with the mission, goals, and objectives of the college in an accurate, effective, and timely manner. Marketing permeates the entire organization in all facets of employee, board, and customer relations. The result is the development and refinement of an organizational image that is clear to external and internal publics.

Conforming Requirements	Measurement Strategy	Cost of Nonconformance
1. A current, flexible tactical marketing plan is in place and is implemented throughout the college. This plan includes plans to reach the following markets:		
a. High school market	Percentage of high school graduates who enroll at FVTC based on targets	Loss of state aids and tuition
b. 1-24 year old market	Comparison of unduplicated headcount from previous year based on targets	Student loss x average credit load x tuition costs x state aids
c. 25-54 year old market	Comparison of unduplicated headcount from previous year based on targets	Student loss x average credit load x tuition costs x state aids
d. Business and industry training market	Number of business and industry contracts and dollars generated compared with the previous year	Loss of dollars generated by contracts
e. Avocational and lifelong learning market	Number of avocational course enrollment figures compared to previous year	Loss of tuition cost

Conforming Requirements	Measurement Strategy	Cost of Nonconformance
2. For each instructional and administrative unit, there is a current written marketing plan that supports the district marketing plan.	Instructional Audit North Central Evaluation Yearly Comprehensive District Marketing Tactical Plan	Increased long-term FVTC marketing costs Staff layoffs Program discontinuance Increased cost per FTE
3. The perception of district citizens toward FVTC is favorable.	Yearly Perception Research Study conducted by Research Department North Central Evaluation	Increased long-term FVTC marketing costs
4. Internal and external customers are satisfied with FVTC products and services.	Annual Employer Satisfaction Survey Annual Student Satisfaction Survey Guaranteed Student Satisfaction for business and industry	Increased long-term FVTC marketing costs Cost of retraining
5. Reliable and valid research is incorporated into the marketing process to ensure continued improvement.	Measurement of tactical marketing promotional strategies and reports on results published includes: a. Evening class schedule b. Business and Industry Seminar Catalog c. Advertising-Institutional d. Catalog e. Advertising-Specific Program	Production costs

APPENDIX J

QUALITY ELEMENT
CUSTOMER SERVICE

Quality Element – Customer Service

The key to the success of FVTC is a satisfied customer.*

We owe it to our current customers, graduates, and potential customers to have and maintain a quality image in the community. This image (which is defined by the components of our key elements) must be clearly stated and understood by all our employees.

A total organizational approach that makes quality of service, as perceived by the customer, the number one driving force for the operation of the college is critical.

This organizational approach includes the following three points:

1. Customer-oriented "front line" employees.
2. Management that supports the "front line" employees.
3. Customer-friendly systems—designed for the convenience of the customers.

*Customers include students, staff, board members, community visitors, employers, vendors, etc.

Conforming Requirements	Measurement Strategy	Cost of Nonconformance
1. All customers are greeted and served in a friendly and cordial manner.	Customer Satisfaction Surveys	Loss of Customers
2. All customers have opportunities to evaluate the instruction and services from the customer's perspective.	Customer Satisfaction Surveys Instructional Audits	
3. All FVTC faculty and staff are continuously inserviced in all aspects of customer service from the customer's perspective.	Inservice program agendas Inservice program evaluation data	
4. All customer complaints and concerns are handled quickly and efficiently via established processes.	File of grievances, ECR forms, CA reports, customer complaints Suggestion box system	

Conforming Requirements	Measurement Strategy	Cost of Nonconformance
5. All faculty and staff know and are trained on the scope of services available at FVTC.	Orientation program agendas Inservice program agenda and evaluation data	Loss of Customers
6. Every courtesy and support is given to internal customers; they in turn can give the best quality service to external customers.	Customer Satisfaction Surveys	
7. Customer service and satisfaction are continuously monitored, evaluated, and measured in an effort toward constant improvement.	Satisfaction Surveys Organizational Climate Surveys	
8. Customer Service Committee reviews customer satisfaction documentation and makes recommendations to the TQLC.	Committee Minutes Customer Satisfaction Surveys	
9. Each service department of the school develops conforming requirements specific to the customers they serve.	List of Conforming Requirements in each department Customer Satisfaction Surveys	

Appendix K

Quality Element
Quality-Based Manager

Quality Element – Quality-Based Manager

Management at FVTC is an ongoing, proactive, problem-solving leadership development process. A person who fulfills the management role in this organization is first a coach and facilitator of people; second a manager of things and events. This person will establish and nurture a creative climate, built on trust, where all members of the team are self-motivated toward the continual success, satisfaction, and improvement of employees, customers, self, and organization to fulfill the college's mission.

Conforming Requirements	Measurement Strategy	Cost of Nonconformance	Benefits of Conformance
1. Demonstrates effective communication skills: Listening Oral Written Interpersonal	To be determined by the team within defined time lines	People stop growing Rework Problems are not identified Lack of commitment and loyalty Fear and victimization Rebellion Dissatisfied customers (inaccurate or late output)	Tasks done right the first time Greater self-expression Climate of trust and openness Respect for each other Clearly defined roles and functions Information sharing equally Deadlines met Time lines of problem solving
2. Is accessible to coworkers.	To be determined by the team within defined time lines	Workers will not change Loss of creativity Communication breaks down Lack of growth Organization will not change Loss of enthusiasm Resentment Frustration	Increased opportunities for communication Willingness to deal with real issues realistically Ability to confront conflict People are allowed to have differences and still function creatively Time becomes available for everyone

Conforming Requirements	Measurement Strategy	Cost of Nonconformance	Benefits of Conformance
3. Makes it possible for people to succeed/help all to become winners.	To be determined by the team within defined time lines	Loss of trust Lack of growth Lack of loyalty and commitment Low morale Lack of retention of staff	Empowerment Self-actualization Solid recognition (beyond "gold watch" or coffee cup) People committed to professional and personal development Individual talents are nurtured Decisions made by those affected
4. De-stresses the office: Is sensitive and tuned in Understands human behavior	To be determined by the team within defined time lines	Anger Ulcers Headaches Absences Forgetfulness Burnout Dissatisfied customers	Teamwork and cooperation Deadlines are met Climate of openness and trust Increased communication
5. Gives and accepts feedback.	To be determined by the team within defined time lines	Continued game playing and "old boy" networks Increased employee frustration Loss of communication Lack of growth and creativity Reduced staff retention	Clear expectations Risks are able to be taken without fear of 'reprisal Networks replace line-and-staff charts Increased employee self-esteem Growth occurs through coaching Understanding Increased flow of communication by all means, including face to face

Conforming Requirements	Measurement Strategy	Cost of Nonconformance	Benefits of Conformance
6. Is adaptable to change.	To be determined by the team within defined time lines	Increased errors and rework Mismatch of persons and jobs Confusion Down time Lack of commitment Efficiency is stifled	Collaborative relations Innovative leadership Issue-based problem solving The unexpected innovations are welcomed and dealt with positively Flexibility to cooperate across division lines rather than to compete
7. Plans ahead.	To be determined by the team within defined time lines	Crisis management Reactive vs. proactive planning Deadlines are not met Down time Poor public relations	Crises are anticipated Contingency plans are in place People are cross-trained Long-range realistic planning Clear goals and objectives Process for solving problems is in place
8. Confronts the need to improve as a leader/motivator: Sets personal and professional goals Professional growth oriented	To be determined by the team within defined time lines	Lack of personal and professional growth Organization will not change Problems will not be solved Atmosphere becomes stagnant	Operates realistically Resources and time for professional and personal development Clear personal goals and values Clear direction and commitment Continued growth/stimulation
9. Follows through in a timely and thorough manner.	To be determined by the team within defined time lines	Lack of involvement Missed deadlines Increased anxiety and stress Resentment Lack of cooperation and trust No action taken	Promises are kept Appropriate and timely action Increased communication Jobs get done right the first time Employee ownership

Conforming Requirements	Measurement Strategy	Cost of Nonconformance	Benefits of Conformance
10. Delegates effectively.	To be determined by the team within defined time lines	People don't know what's expected Communication breaks down Overloads People's talents are under or overtaxed	Obstacles to drift removed Independence encourages teamwork and reciprocal support of all members Individual talents used to potential Shared leadership and decision making
11. Demonstrates positive leadership: Ethical Honest Consistent Fair Knowledgeable decision making	To be determined by the team within defined time lines	Communication breaks down Loss of cooperation and commitment Fear Lack of trust Lack of growth Continuation of political "old boy" network	Top down example set in all interactions Win-win negotiations Loyalty and commitment Higher staff retention Increases communication Equitable problem-solving processes implemented Trust

Appendix L

Evaluation Plan

Key Studies	1990-91	1991–92	1992–93
Monthly:			
Indicators of District Health	X	X	X
Yearly:			
Graduate Follow-Up – 6 mo.	X	X	X
Mini-Audit/Screening	X	X	X
Instructional Audits	1 – Truck Driving 2 – Farm Operations 3 – Farm Business and Production 4 – Account Assistant 5 – Office Assistant 6 – Hospitality Management		
Service Unit Audits	1 – Curriculum Services 2 – Financial Services		
Regional Study	Wautoma		
New Program Needs Assessments	1 – Direct Marketing 2 – Hospitality/Program Expansion 3 – Nursing Program Expansion		
Every 2 years:			
Climate Survey		X	
Student Satisfaction	X		X
Employer Survey		X	
Every 3–4 years:			
Perception Survey			X
Graduate Follow-Up – 5 yr.		X	
Special One-Time			
CIM Evaluation	X		
Lifetime Planning Center Research Project	X		
GOAL Follow-Up Study	X		

APPENDIX M

COSTS OF CONFORMANCE 1987–1988

Cost of Conformance	Itemized Costs	
1.10 Marketing Research		$ 26,554
(Based upon 50 percent of Research Department budget)		
1.11 Labor	$ 22,030	
1.12 Printing	1,032	
1.13 Mailing and supplies	3,492	
1.20 Quality Orientation and Training		68,805
(Based upon actual costs except staff time)		
1.21 Labor (Instructor)	27,951	
1.22 Instructional materials	20,410	
1.23 Workshops and conferences	20,444	
1.30 Quality First Process Coordination		43,707
(Based upon actual costs)		
1.31 Labor (coordination)	27,259	
1.32 Supplies and materials	1,425	
1.33 Research design costs	15,023	
1.40 Quality Monitoring and Auditing		26,554
(Based upon 50 percent of Research Department budget)		
1.41 Labor	22,030	
1.42 Printing	1,032	
1.43 Mailing and supplies	3,492	
1.50 Wellness Program		6,439
(Based upon costs of operation)		
1.51 Labor	5,905	
1.52 Supplies and materials	534	
TOTAL COST OF CONFORMANCE		**$172,059**

COSTS OF NONCONFORMANCE 1987–1988

2.10 **Resource Utilization/Enrollments**

(Based upon percentage of maximum enrollments)

2.11 Direction instruction $3,497,336

1,850,032

	Enrollment	Capacity	Direct Cost	
Business enrollment	713	895	$ 2,354,753	$ 478,844
General Education enrollment	870	1,070	3,294,182	615,735
Health and Human Services enrollment	790	887	2,689,274	294,092
Technical enrollment	1,060	1,181	3,330,313	341,209
Oshkosh enrollment	301	348	605,494	81,776
Economic Development enrollment	89	106	239,283	38,376
	3,823	4,487	$12,513,299	$1,850,032

Division Overhead $ 257,190

2.12

	Division Cost	Division Idle Capacity	
Business enrollment	$ 401,161	20.34%	$ 81,577
General Education enrollment	173,286	18.69%	32,390
Health and Human Services enrollment	692,890	10.94%	75,773
Technical enrollment	472,216	10.25%	48,381
Oshkosh enrollment	85,134	13.51%	11,498
Economic Development enrollment	47,213	16.04%	7,572
	$1,871,900		

2.13 Institutional Overhead   75.14% $1,390,114

2.20 **Rework in Service Departments**

(Based upon 20% of service department budgets or actual) $1,138,365

2.21 Labor to correct $ 961,101

2.22 Machine time   135,478

2.23 Supplies   41,786

$1,138,365

2.30 **Retention of Students** $2,156,000
      (Based on FTE loss times state aids/tuition)

	FTEs		
Business dropouts	220.00		
General Education dropouts	264.00		
Health and Human Services dropouts	218.00		
Technical dropouts	286.00		
Oshkosh dropouts	88.00		
Economic Development dropouts	2.0		
	1,078.00		

2.31 Loss of state aids		900.00	970,200
2.32 Loss of tuition		1,100.00	1,185,800

2.40 **Employee Attendance** $ 382,115
      (Based upon loss of time above 1.8% of total time available)

2.41 Overtime due to absence	$18,497,537	1.80%	332,956
2.42 Substitutes	49,159		49,159

2.50 **Scheduling of Human Resources** $ 924,877
      (Based upon 5% of labor costs)

2.51 Actual labor	$18,497,537	5.00%	924,877

2.60 **Customer Service** $ 25,578
      (Based upon actual time handling complaints–initial estimate one employee)

2.61 Reports and correspondence	$25,578		25,578

                        TOTAL COST OF NONCONFORMANCE   **$8,124,270**

APPENDIX O

SUMMARY OF EXTERNAL QUALITY AUDIT

On April 25-26, 1990, an external audit team visited FVTC to investigate our progress with the Quality First Process. In their day and a half at FVTC, the team interviewed staff and reviewed documents connected with the quality process, including the Quality Process Survey. At the conclusion of their visit, the team gave their opinion of conforming requirements of the 15 steps of Quality First. Their ratings and comments are detailed in the On-Site Review section of this report. In addition, the team gave an oral summary of their observations.

Summary Statements

Staff are extremely committed to the mission of FVTC, which is to educate students for employment. A wide range of positive comments about FVTC reflected staff dedication to the school's purpose. Furthermore, staff sincerely want to participate in a quality process. They showed a strong desire to see FVTC succeed with quality. Staff training to date has provided a good foundation in the quality process; however, the staff need further training to acquire the tools such as statistical skills and team skills to integrate quality into their work settings.

The effort FVTC has put into quality is commendable, particularly considering there is no final word on the best way to implement quality in an educational setting. No school is as far along as FVTC in the quality process. Most educational institutions would "score zero" on every quality attribute in this audit.

At the present stage, we suggest concentrating on integrating quality into daily activities of staff and getting it to be a way of life. Measurement, really the scientific method, should be a way of investigating and analyzing what is occurring in the work units. The TQLC's short-term goal is to facilitate the quality process, but its long-term goal should be to work itself "out of business." Overall, more flexibility in the quality process is needed—we doubt that you can "march to quality" with a cookbook approach.

We suggest reevaluating certain quality concepts and terms. Terms that have negative connotations should be reconsidered and perhaps replaced. The quality steps and committees should be reevaluated to see whether they are truly needed. For example, the CPI (Continuous Process Improvement), as part of the CPI step, should be redirected from a blame-ridden system to become a nonthreatening method of solving problems. Conformance to requirements should not be viewed as an end goal; rather, innovation should be encouraged. Reaching optimum levels and going beyond limits, i.e., the concept of continuous improvement, is the key to quality.

FVTC has achieved terrific involvement and success with the outside community. Students know FVTC cares. In interviews, they were extremely positive about the educational environment at FVTC. The focus externally has been excellent. We suggest you now turn your attention to internal matters. Communication of all types needs great improvement. Bottom-up communication needs development—people need to know they are being listened to. Managers, including top administration, should do more speaking and less writing and offer more demonstration of the quality process. Individuals need to see how the quality process might benefit them. Quality should be fun.

Key Recommendations

1. Improve Communication

- Communication should involve more speaking and less writing.
- Inform people of why decisions are made.
- Develop "bottom-up" communication.
- Involve staff with operational planning, the development of the key elements, and quality steps.
- Students should turn in their course evaluations to a third party.

2. Increase Staff Training

- Individuals need help to understand the benefits of participation in the quality process. Quality should be fun.
- Provide training to supply the staff with the tools they need to implement quality, including statistical skills, team skills, how to develop a training plan for a unit, and other related activities.
- Increase emphasis on making data-based decisions at the work unit level.
- Use measurement as a way of investigating and analyzing what is occurring in the work units.
- Conduct the educational training needs survey as planned.

- Teach the staff how to access the bulletin board once they have signed on.

3. Integrate Quality into Staff's Work Life

- Top administration should demonstrate the quality process to the staff.
- Quality should be integrated into FVTC staff's everyday activities and job descriptions.
- Some team members felt that in the future quality should be integrated into agenda items and budget items.
- The TQLC should 1) provide leadership, 2) motivate, 3) facilitate, and 4) coordinate. With these four items as their top priorities, the TQLC would eventually be out of business.

4. Reevaluate Certain Quality Concepts

- Consider replacing certain terms that may have negative connotations.
- Define what the true quality characteristics are for internal and external customers.
- The quality steps and related committees should be evaluated to determine whether or not they are needed.
- Costing of quality should be de-emphasized in the measurement of the quality process.
- Conforming requirements should not function as an end goal for achieving quality.
- Be more flexible in application of the quality concepts.
- Encourage innovation rather than emphasizing conformance to requirements.
- Redirect the intent of the CPI.
- The TQLC should monitor its action plans.

5. Address Human Resource Issues

- Develop a process for assuring continuity of the Quality Coordinator's job from one year to the next.
- Promote advisory committee members' leadership in committee activities and program direction.
- Clarify the position responsibilities of the CPI coordinator.
- Provide the CPI Committee the authority to make the process more effective.
- Team facilitators should be selected by team members rather than appointed.

Appendix P

Malcolm Baldrige Examination Categories

1990 Examination Categories/Items	Maximum Points	Fox Valley Self-Analysis
1.0 Leadership	**100**	____
1.1 Senior Executive Leadership	30	____
1.2 Quality Values	20	____
1.3 Management for Quality	30	____
1.4 Public Responsibility	20	____
2.0 Information and Analysis	**60**	____
2.1 Scope and Management of Quality Data and Information	35	____
2.2 Analysis of Quality Data and Information	25	____
3.0 Strategic Quality Planning	**90**	____
3.1 Strategic Quality Planning Process	40	____
3.2 Quality Leadership Indicators in Planning	25	____
3.3 Quality Priorities	25	____
4.0 Human Resource Utilization	**150**	____
4.1 Human Resource Management	30	____
4.2 Employee Involvement	40	____
4.3 Quality Education and Training	40	____
4.4 Employee Recognition and Performance Measurement	20	____
4.5 Employee Well-Being and Morale	20	____
5.0 Assurance of Products and Services	**150**	____
5.1 Design and Introduction of Quality Products and Services	30	____
5.2 Process and Quality Control	25	____
5.3 Continuous Improvement of Processes, Products and Services	25	____
5.4 Quality Assessment	15	____
5.5 Documentation	10	____
5.6 Quality Assurance, Quality Assessment and Quality Improvement of Support Services and Business Processes	25	____
5.7 Quality Assurance, Quality Assessment and Quality Improvement of Suppliers	20	____
6.0 Quality Results	**150**	____
6.1 Quality of Products and Services	50	____
6.2 Comparison of Quality Results	35	____
6.3 Business Process, Operational and Support Service Quality Improvement	35	____
6.4 Supplier Quality Improvement	30	____

7.0 Customer Satisfaction   **300**   _____

    7.1 Knowledge of Customer Requirements and Expectations   50   _____
    7.2 Customer Relationship Management   30   _____
    7.3 Customer Service Standards   20   _____
    7.4 Commitment to Customers   20   _____
    7.5 Complaint Resolution for Quality Improvement   30   _____
    7.6 Customer Satisfaction Determination   50   _____
    7.7 Customer Satisfaction Results   50   _____
    7.8 Customer Satisfaction Comparison   50   _____

    Total Points   **1000**   _____

Appendix Q

1990–1991 Operational Thrusts

1. Implement the FVTC Cost Containment Plan using the quality process with major emphasis on:

   - Recruitment, retention, and placement
   - Measurement and costing
   - Customer satisfaction
   - Faculty/Staff education and training

2. Study and implement new programs and processes related to the use and enhancement of Human Resources:

   - Design of individualized professional and personal growth plans
   - Analysis of the roles and functions of all those involved in the instructional process including faculty and managers
   - Design of new systems of management organization and compensation

3. Analyze the instructional development and evaluation process in order to improve support services for faculty/staff.

4. Develop new instructional programs as follows:

   - Aeronautics/Pilot technology
   - Avionics technician
   - Airframe Mechanics
   - Powerplant Mechanics
   - Insurance Service Specialist
   - Alcohol and Other Drug Abuse
   - Quality Process Technician
   - Landscape Construction/Maintenance

- Advanced Technical Certificates
  - Business Applications in CIM
  - Technical Applications in CIM
  - Manufacturing Technologies Center
  - PC CAD Applications

5. Enhance the management and operation of the district through the design of new and improved management information systems, including the implementation of the recommendations of the Applied Technology Study (ATS).

6. Focus on the initiation of training in Computer Integrated Manufacturing (CIM) for business and industry.

7. Complete plans and specifications of the Oshkosh Aviation Center, Regional Fire Training Center, and the expansion of the WDDC.

SURVEY OF ORGANIZATIONS 2000

Used with Permission of Rensis Likert & Associates

Sample Questions

	To a very little extent	To a little extent	To some extent	To a great extent	To a very great extent
4. In this organization, to what extent are decisions made at those levels where the most adequate and accurate information is available?	1	2	3	4	5
7. How receptive are people *above your supervisor* to ideas and suggestions coming from your work group?	1	2	3	4	5
11. When decisions are being made, to what extent are the persons affected asked for their ideas?	1	2	3	4	5
How friendly and easy to approach is your supervisor?					
24. This is how it is *now*	1	2	3	4	5
25. This is how I'd *like* it to be	1	2	3	4	5
To what extent does your supervisor provide help, training, and guidance so that you can improve your performance?					
38. This is how it is *now*	1	2	3	4	5
39. This is how I'd *like* it to be	1	2	3	4	5
48. To what extent does your supervisor have knowledge of what it takes to be a good leader?	1	2	3	4	5
50. To what extent does your supervisor have skills for getting along with others?	1	2	3	4	5
58. To what extent is *your work group efficient* in doing the work that is expected of it?	1	2	3	4	5
How friendly and easy to approach are the persons in your work group?					
60. This is how it is *now*	1	2	3	4	5
61. This is how I'd *like* it to be	1	2	3	4	5
83. To what extent does your work group make good decisions and solve problems well?	1	2	3	4	5

APPENDIX S

NEW PARADIGMS
CURRICULUM AND INSTRUCTION

Old Paradigm	New (FVTC) Paradigm
• Curriculum is based on textbooks, teacher experiences, and untested content.	• Curriculum is based on job tasks which are converted to competencies which must be mastered.
• The plan for learning is unorganized, outdated, and incomplete.	• There is a complete, computerized plan for learning for each course, which is updated regularly.
• Students must repeat competencies which they have already mastered.	• Students receive credit for past experience in occupations or in education.
• Students may enter only once or twice a year and must graduate en masse without regard for time of mastery of course requirements.	• There is a multiple entry/ multiple exit system which enables students to enroll at various times and graduate when requirements have been met.
• The continuum for learning is disjointed because there is little or no articulation between the educational levels.	• There is a lifetime learning sequence in place which begins in high school, continues at the 2-year college, and advances through university education.
• Training for business and industry design is based on full-time courses and programs.	• Curriculum used in business and industry is customized to meet the needs of the employees.

Old Paradigm	New (FVTC) Paradigm
• Most learning/teaching is instructor directed in a self-contained classroom/laboratory.	• A variety of teaching methods are used in order to match student learning styles.
• Since there are no pre-requisites and entrance testing requirements, students select courses based on their individual desires without adequate counseling and advisement.	• Course prerequisites are established and students are counseled into regular, developmental, or advanced courses based on their best achievements as measured during entrance teaching.
• Advisory committees are lacking or are inactive and ineffective.	• Advisory committees are active and assist in program development, implementation, and evaluation.
• There is little contact with businesses and industries which are related to the occupational programs.	• Each program includes a business/industry collaboration component, such as work experience, related to the training.
• Examinations are designed without a direct link to course objectives.	• Criterion-referenced examinations measure mastery of competencies.
• Evaluation is unorganized, unscheduled, and without a focus on improvement.	• An effective system of continuous evaluation exists in the following format: – Instructional Audits – Student Satisfaction Surveys – Employer Satisfaction Surveys – Faculty Evaluation Systems
• Equipment is outdated and inappropriate, and computer usage by students is limited.	• Students use state-of-the-art equipment and technology, with specific emphasis on computer competence.

Old Paradigm	New (FVTC) Paradigm

• All classes and laboratory sessions are highly structured and operating on time requirements with uniform class development.

• Instruction is teacher directed, controlled, and without active involvement by students.

• Individualized learning laboratories with several teaching/learning methods are available at times which are convenient to students.

• Students are responsible for learning under the guidance and management of the instructor. Learning is fun.

APPENDIX T

NEW PARADIGMS
HUMAN RESOURCES

Old Paradigm	New (FVTC) Paradigm
• Professional development plan is unorganized with inadequate resources.	• For each full-time employee, there is a Professional/ Personal Development plan and profile. The overall organizational plan has a budget of at least 2% of total budget.
• Recruitment and selection activities are unorganized and ineffective.	• Recruitment activities are organized and selection techniques are systematized in order to attract and attain competent employees.
• Inequities occur in the way persons are hired or promoted.	• Equal opportunities exist for all applicants and employees which meet and exceed statute requirements.
• No employee feedback is solicited.	• Employees have regular opportunities to complete confidential organizational climate surveys which are analyzed and given top-level attention.
	• All levels of personnel have opportunities for input into work unit decision making.
• There are problems related to cleanliness, safety, and health practices due to a lack of organized processes.	• Physical facilities are attractive, clean and neat, and exceed health and safety standards.

Old Paradigm	New (FVTC) Paradigm
• Constant conflicts occur between union and management.	• There is active involvement of unions in strategic decision making.
• There are constant grievances, hearings, disciplinary meetings, and ineffective negotiations between management and unions.	• Both bargaining parties assume that they have common problems and that solutions are possible to benefit all. "Win-win" bargaining is used.
• Traditional forms and assumptions of adversarial labor relations lead to poor morale and constant staff problems.	• The work climate fosters management and unions working together to increase productivity and improve employee well-being by having process oriented and problem solving management systems.
• Jobs are designed by managers without much input by the employee.	• Employees are involved in job design and job enrichment by assisting in establishing new job structures and flexible schedules.
• Information is reserved for only a few top managers.	• Crucial information, data, and reports are made available to unions following confidentiality requirements.
	• Management takes responsibility for protecting union security. Unions do not infringe on areas left within management jurisdiction.
• Poor communication exists throughout the organization.	• There is constant communication at all levels of the organization which focuses on face-to-face discussions. It requires using language employees can understand and listening to customers.

Old Paradigm	New (FVTC) Paradigm
• There is no formal employee recognition program.	• Employee recognition programs which are comprehensive and individualized are in place and are monitored.
• Employees are discouraged from trying new ways to do things.	• There are opportunities for innovation and experimentation with a tolerance for risk taking and an acceptance of failure.
• Management believes that wellness programs are the total responsibility of the individual.	• Employees are encouraged to participate in an organized wellness program which is available and accessible.
• There are high turnover rates at all levels of the school.	• Employee turnover rates are less than the national and local averages.

APPENDIX U

NEW PARADIGMS
CUSTOMER SERVICES

Old Paradigm	New (FVTC) Paradigm
• Entrance assessments are lacking or are not used in counseling and advising students.	• Students receive entrance assessments, counseling, and advisement in order to make appropriate occupational choices.
• Students are not treated as customers.	• Students are greeted and serviced in a friendly, helpful way.
• Students complaints are handled in a defensive and negative way.	• Customer (student) complaints are handled quickly and efficiently.
• Many students graduate and are unable to find jobs in their area of training.	• Students who graduate are guaranteed retraining if they are unable to get a job in their field of training.
• Students are not encouraged to offer suggestions or voice complaints.	• There is an ongoing system to enable students to offer suggestions, voice complaints, and assist in making their experiences more worthwhile.
• Service department staff do not treat other employees or students as customers.	• Each service department establishes customer satisfaction conforming requirements.
• There is no adequate follow-up system for students and graduates.	• There is a follow-up plan to track placement of graduates, attrition rates, and job advancement.

Old Paradigm	New (FVTC) Paradigm
• There are no special courses or programs to assist new students in adjusting to college life.	• There is a special orientation program including "college survival" courses available to all students.
• Students are looked upon as being inferior and they are not treated in a respectful, considerate, and friendly way.	• Customers are treated with politeness, respect, consideration, and friendliness by contact persons including receptionists and telephone operators.
• There is a lack of willingness and readiness to provide accessible student services which meet student requirements.	• Student services staff are responsive through a willingness and readiness to provide service which is accessible to customers and exceeds their expectations.

APPENDIX V

NEW PARADIGMS
MANAGEMENT/ADMINISTRATION

Old Paradigm	New (FVTC) Paradigm
• The school is structured with typical hierarchical structures and with several layers of channels.	• Horizontal structures are replacing hierarchical organizational charts with several layers of channels.
• The focus is on management of things and control over employees, systems, and operations.	• The focus is on leadership skills such as empowerment, involvement, and enablement rather than on management of things.
• Most decisions are made without input by employees	• Managers actively promote teamwork and problem solving within their work units.
• The plans and budgets are developed by a few top level administrators.	• Individuals at all levels of the organization are involved in the planning process and are surveyed to identify their needs and priorities.
• The plan is developed, distributed to staff, and put on the shelf.	• The operational plans of the departments are linked inseparably to the budgeting of resources.
• There are no contingency plans to cope with downturns in resources.	• There is a written cost containment plan which is updated annually.

Old Paradigm	New (FVTC) Paradigm
• Program, staff, and facility plans are short term without regard for establishing priorities.	• The planning process is continuous (year-round) and flexible enough to be dynamic and responsive with a long-range plan for programming, staffing, and facility construction and renovation.
• Computer reports are inaccurate, incomplete, and virtually useless.	• Technology is utilized and support services are organized to produce concise reports, documents, communications, and schedules.
• There is an overabundance of paper documents, reports, and memoranda.	• Hard copy documentation is significantly reduced through electronic data generation.
• The information system is outdated and not useful to help manage the system.	• Computerized record keeping systems monitor student enrollment, progress, and performance.
	• The information system produces enough meaningful reports to adequately assist managers and instructors
• The district marketing plan is outdated and not documented.	• There is a current written marketing plan in place which identifies target markets and outlines strategies to maximize enrollments.
• There is little or no research related to marketing.	• Reliable and valid research is incorporated into the marketing process.

Old Paradigm	New (FVTC) Paradigm
• Most decisions are made on the spur of the moment by a few managers or a single manager with no quantifiable factual basis.	• There is a statistical thinking philosophy which permeates the school and requires the use of valid data for problem solving and decision making.
• The District Director/President and senior Vice Presidents give lip service to the quality process but don't practice what they preach.	• The College Director/President, the senior Vice Presidents, and middle managers are all committed to the quality process through demonstrated adherence to the principles of total quality management.
• Meetings are poorly organized, start late, last too long, and are classical bores to most participants.	• Meetings are planned, conducted, and reported following established policies for efficient and effective meetings.
• There is no system of accountability linked to staff and building utilization and costs of doing things.	• There is an agreed upon system of accountability and productivity through the establishment and monitoring of: – Class Sizes – Instructor Work Loads – Facility Utilization • There is an ongoing plan for determining the costs related to quality including: – Costs of Conformance – Costs of Nonconformance

ENDNOTES

1. Perry, Nancy J., "Saving in the Schools—How Business Can Help," *Fortune*, November 7, 1988.

2. Spanbauer, Stanley J., *Quality First in Education...Why Not?*, Fox Valley Technical College Foundation, Appleton, Wisconsin, 1987.

3. "Improving the Business of Education," Center for Work Force Preparation and Quality Education, U.S. Chamber of Commerce, 1990, pp. 1-15.

4. Patterson, Jerry L., Purkey, Stewart, and Parker, Jackson, "Productive School Systems for a Nonrational World," *ASCD*, Alexandria, Virginia, 1986.

5. Paulu, Nancy, "Key Player in School Reform; The Superintendent," *The School Administrator*, March 1989, pp. 8-14.

6. Juran, Joseph and Gryna, F. M., "Policies and Objectives," *Quality Planning and Analysis*, McGraw-Hill, New York, 1980, p. 545.

7. Grant, David, "Being an Effective Member of a Work Group," Dartnell, Chicago, Illinois, 1989.

8. Goodman, John, "The Nature of Customer Satisfaction," *Quality Progress*, February 1989, pp. 37-38.

9. Ibid., pp. 38-40.

10. Hutchins, Spencer Jr., "What Customers Want: Results of ASQC/Gallup Poll," *Quality Progress*, October 1989, pp. 33-35.

11. "Competitive Benchmarking: What It Is and What It Can Do for You," Xerox Corporation, 1987, pp. 2-3.

12. Parasuraman, Zeithami, and Berry, *Journal of Marketing*, Fall 1985.

13. '88 Gallup Survey, "Consumers' Perceptions Concerning the Quality of American Products and Services," ASQC, 1988, p. 23.

14. *Connections*, The Noel/Levitz Customer Service Training Program, Better Than Money Corporation, Bloomington, Minnesota, 1988.

15. Futrell, Mary Hatwood, "NEA Undergirds Bottom-up Change," *The School Administrator*, February 1989, p. 64.

16. Peters, Tom, *Thriving on Chaos*, Knopf, New York, 1987.

17. Perry, Nancy J., op. cit., pp. 42-46.

18. Spanbauer, Stanley J., op. cit., pp. 23-52.

19. "School-Based Management—A Strategy for Better Learning," American Association for School Administrators, National Association of Elementary School Principals, and National Association of Secondary School Principals, 1988, p. 6.

20. Bradford, David L. and Cohen, Allan R., *Managing for Excellence*, John Wiley and Sons, New York, 1984.

21. Boyer, Ernest, "Vital Statistics," *The American School Board Journal*, January 1989.

22. Casanova, Ursula, "Research and Practice: We Can Integrate Them," *Researching Teachers*, January 1989, pp. 49-50.

23. Albrecht, Karl, *At America's Service*, Dow Jones-Irwin, Homewood, Illinois, 1988, pp. 14-16.

24. *Solving Quality and Productivity Problems: Goodmeasure's Guide to Corrective Action*, Staff of Goodmeasure, Inc., ASQC Quality Press, Milwaukee, Wisconsin, 1988, pp. 89, 124-127.

25. Manz, Charles C. and Sims, Henry P. Jr., "Leading Workers to Lead Themselves: The External Leadership of Self-Management Work Team," *Administrative Science Quarterly*, 32 (1987): pp. 106-128.

26. *A Nation Prepared: Teachers for the 21st Century*, Task Force on Teaching as a Profession of the Carnegie Forum on Education and the Economy, Carnegie Corporation, New York, New York, May 1986.

27. Futrell, Mary Hatwood, "Restructuring Teaching: A Call for Research," *Education Week*, September 1987, pp. 2-5.

28. Levis, Anne, *Restructuring America's Schools*, American Association of School Administrators, Arlington, Virginia, 1989, pp. 84-86.

29. Bednarczyk, Betty L., Negus, David P., and Persico, John, "The Role of the Union, Management, and Consultant in a Total Quality Transformation Effort," ASQC Quality Congress Transactions, Toronto, 1989.

30. Baker, George A. III, Roueche, John E., and Gillett-Karam, Rosemary, *Teaching As Leading: Profiles of Excellence in the Open-Door College*, The Community College Press, AACJC, 1990.

31. Ibid., pp. 117-143.

32. Rosander, A. C., *The Quest for Quality in Services*, Quality Press, American Society for Quality Control, Milwaukee, 1989, pp. 41-47.

33. Ibid., pp. 50-56.

34. Scholtes, Peter R. and others, *The Team Handbook*, Joiner Associates, Inc., Madison, Wisconsin, 1988, pp. 5-9, 5-11.

35. Deming, W. Edwards, *Out of Crisis*, Massachusetts Institute of Technology, Center for Advanced Engineering Study, Boston, Massachusetts, 1986, pp. 318-369.

36. Ishikawa, Kaoru, *Guide to Quality Control*, Asian Productivity Organization, UNIPUB, New York, New York, 1976, p. 180.

37. *Transformation of American Industry Training Systems*, Productivity-Quality Systems, Inc., Dayton, Ohio, p. 197.

38. Scherkenbach, William W., *The Deming Route to Quality and Productivity*, Mercury Press, Rockville, Maryland, 1986, p. 212.

39. "Quality Elements," Fox Valley Technical College, February 1991.

40. Zimmerman, Catherine, "A Report to Determine Sales Factors Which Impact Most on the Income of the Oshkosh Campus," October 1990.

41. Noordyk, Virgil, "A Project to Determine Which Technical Division Programs Should Be Offered During the Summer Block in 1991," November 1990.

42. *Principles of Quality Costs*, American Society for Quality Control Quality Costs Committee, Campanella, Jack (Chairman), Hagan, John T. (Editor), American Society for Quality Control, Milwaukee, Wisconsin, 1987, p. 203.

43. "1990 Application Guidelines," *Malcolm Baldrige National Quality Award*, U.S. Department of Commerce, National Institute of Standards and Technology, 1990.

44. Ibid., pp. 17-23.

INDEX